D1304797

PAPERCRAFT PROJECTS WITH ONE PIECE OF PAPER

MICHAEL GRATER

Line Illustrations by the Author

Photographs by Geoffrey Goode

DOVER PUBLICATIONS, INC.

NEW YORK

Published in Canada by General Publishing Company, Ltd., 30 Lesmill Road, Don Mills, Toronto, Ontario.
Published in the United Kingdom by Constable and Company, Ltd.

This Dover edition, first published in 1987, is an unabridged republication of the work first published by Mills & Boon Limited, London, 1963, under the title *One Piece of Paper: For Children and for Teachers*. The present edition includes one correction and one addition by the author, as well as a new Note to the Dover Edition discussing paper sizes.

Manufactured in the United States of America
Dover Publications, Inc., 31 East 2nd Street, Mineola, N.Y. 11501

Library of Congress Cataloging-in-Publication Data

Grater, Michael, 1923–
    Papercraft projects with one piece of paper.

    Reprint. Originally published: One piece of paper. London : Mills & Boon, 1963.
    Summary: Introduces techniques for making animals, faces, and geometric shapes out of paper.
    1. Paper sculpture—Juvenile literature. [1. Paper sculpture. 2. Paper work. 3. Sculpture. 4. Handicraft] I. Goode, Geoffrey, ill. II. Title.
TT870.G688 1987   736'.98   87-19938
ISBN 0-486-25504-2 (pbk.)

NOTE TO THE DOVER EDITION

The British terms for paper sizes used in this book now need clarification for readers in Britain as well as in America, because Britain has changed over to International paper sizes (A0 to A7).

The terms that occur most frequently in the text are Imperial, Half Imperial and Quarter Imperial. At its first appearance, each of these terms is immediately followed by its equivalent in inches, but a handy summary here may not be out of place:

> Imperial: 30 × 22 inches.
> Half Imperial: 22 × 15 inches.
> Quarter Imperial: 15 × 11 inches.

Note that on pages 46, 89 and 105, "Half Imperial" really refers to half of an Imperial sheet (30 × 11 inches.)

In the International nomenclature, the nearest size to Imperial is A1 (841 × 594 mm; 33.1 × 23.4 inches). Nearest to Half Imperial is A2 (594 × 420 mm; 23.4 × 16.5 inches). Nearest to Quarter Imperial is A3 (420 × 297 mm; 16.5 × 11.7 inches). The "one third Imperial" on pages 95 and 98 (22 × 10 inches) can be adapted from an A1 or an A2 sheet. The "one eighth Imperial" on page 101 (11 × 7½ inches) is closest to the A4 size (297 × 210 mm; 11.7 × 8.3 inches).

Moreover, the terms for types of paper (Cartridge, Sugar) used here may not be familiar, but substitutions in these cases will be obvious.

CONTENTS

	Page
INTRODUCTION	9
MATERIALS	13
TECHNIQUES	15
SCORING AND FOLDING	15
Witches	17
Mice	20
Animals with an Ark	22
Standing Figures	24
Nativity	26
CURVING THE SCORE	29
Fish	30
Caterpillars	32
CUT TO CENTRE	33
Fireworks	34
Faces and Portraits	35
CURLING	39
FORMS FROM ONE PIECE OF PAPER	42
Lizard	42
Fly	47
Seagull	51
Seahorse	55
Owl	59
Frog (1)	62
Frog (2)	66
Rabbit	69
Woodpecker (1)	72
Woodpecker (2)	75
Swift	80
Fish	84
Shark	89
Roundabout Horse	92
Crocodile	95
Tortoise	98
Mouse	101
Rat	105
Angel	108
Butterfly	111
CONCLUSION	115
FOR TEACHERS	116

INTRODUCTION

In a previous book on Paper Sculpture I introduced children and teachers to some of the ways in which a flat piece of paper can be made to assume various interesting shapes.

Many of the children and their teachers were surprised – and some were even delighted – to discover exciting and unexpected shapes hidden away in ordinary pieces of paper. There were caterpillars which ended up crawling over classroom ceilings, while birds and fish floated across the room. The shapes were often colourful and exciting, and it was clear that many of the children introduced to the subject were enjoying the practical work involved.

The present volume is intended to stimulate and further assist children and teachers who have already played with paper. It might also interest those who come to the craft for the first time.

In preparing it I have selected and illustrated a few of the shapes which are hiding somewhere in any flat piece of paper. The examples vary mainly between animals, birds, fish and insects, and although they are all different, they all have one thing in common. They can all be found in – or made from – one piece of paper.

For the benefit of anyone coming to the craft for the first time I have included a brief practical introduction to the simple – but necessary – techniques of paper sculpture. These techniques, or methods of handling paper, can be mastered by anyone who has never previously worked in the craft, by attempting the exercises in the order suggested. In this way anyone who wishes to go on to the later shapes can get a feeling for paper, and can appreciate some of the possibilities and the limitations of the material.

In the process of learning he can also make and see certain simple but entertaining results.

After mastering the simple techniques an interested student should be able to make any of the later shapes for which patterns are given. Those who go on to the shapes are recommended to make a careful study of the pattern, or first diagram, in each example. Although it is not necessary to reproduce this in every case with absolute accuracy, it is desirable to get the general proportions as close as possible to those shown in the diagram.

A suitable size is suggested at the beginning of the instructions for each exercise. This is quoted in terms of an Imperial size sheet (30 inches by 22 inches), which is the size of paper normally available in shops and schools.

Unless it is definitely stated in the instructions it is not necessary to cut papers for the exercises exactly to the sizes given. Most paper sizes can be made by folding and cutting an Imperial sheet, and variations in the original size can be left in the cut piece if they occur.

It is more important to get the right sort of proportions into the exercise. Long thin shapes must remain long and thin, and you must be clear about the way the paper is folded before cutting. If the proportions are not carefully seen in the diagrams, and as carefully reproduced, the end results might be distorted out of all recognition and be unlike the examples illustrated in the photographs.

If you disregard the given proportions and the results are interesting in their own way you will have lost nothing. But if the model is distorted to such an extent that it becomes unsuccessful it will be necessary to return to the proportions shown in the diagram.

When reproducing the pattern on your own paper you can of course use a ruler to establish parts of the diagram in the correct positions. Any method which helps you, or which you find convenient, is permissible. After the diagram has been reproduced the shape can be cut, but care is again necessary at this stage. You should cut as close to the drawn line as is possible. In most cases, as is indicated in the diagrams, the shapes can be cut double with the paper folded through the centre, giving two identical sides.

After cutting, the suggested form (or shape) can be raised by following the instructions stage by stage and by referring, where necessary, to the diagrams which have been included to assist you.

For your further assistance at this stage the position of the eyes is shown, where possible, in each diagram.

If you find at some point in your work that you are not able to make a shape successfully you will probably have misread or misinterpreted a stage in the instructions. This is almost inevitable somewhere in your work, but it should not deter you. Instead of throwing the shape away in disgust you should go back over the processes, checking your original cut against the printed diagram. After ensuring that this is correct you should repeat the making-up process stage by stage until you have found the fault, or have mastered the correct way of manipulating the paper.

Reference to the photographs may in some instances help to overcome a particular difficulty, since the photographs illustrate the type of shape which can be raised from the printed diagram. But the main thing is to work slowly through each process in the development of the shape, making sure that you can understand and are able to follow each instruction.

You should also allow a reasonable amount of time for each work. It is obviously not possible to make all the shapes in one day. To get maximum enjoyment and satisfaction from them you should work on one shape at a time, repeating it if necessary until you can raise the form without referring to the instructions.

When you are able to make a shape — and can undo and put it together again — you can experiment on it with colour and decoration. In this part of the work there are no instructions to follow. You can please yourself.

If you prefer you can paint the models in realistic colours as they would be in real life. But you will have more fun, and will add to your knowledge of colour, if you make your decorations with colours and patterns of your own choice.

Any of the shapes can be used as an opportunity to experiment with colours and patterns. You can either paint them flat or work on them after they have been made up.

In some cases it is useful to start with a piece of paper already prepared in one colour. In a few instances, if you use this method, the paper should be coloured on both sides, since in some models parts of both sides can be seen in the finished form.

When painting any of the models you should take care not to make the paper too wet. You should try to use your colour thick rather than watery, otherwise the paper will tend to curl or bend out of shape. Felt-tips are also recommended.

If you remember that you are working with paper, which is a slightly fragile material, and that you must handle it with a certain care, you will avoid buckling and bending the paper where a bend is not required.

The best and most competent work in paper is that which is crisp and clean, and that which bends or takes a shape only where it is intended to. You should be firm with the paper but you should treat it with care and with concern for its lack of real strength — as you would treat a baby animal.

In this way, if you master the processes involved, working the examples illustrated should give you pleasure. If you do them as well as you are able, and decorate them to your own satisfaction, it will be enough. You will have made a worthwhile effort.

If, in the process of making this effort, you are able to produce interesting shapes with attractive and lively colours and patterns, you will enjoy the work. You might even reach the stage where — starting with one piece of paper — you can produce something which can give amusement and pleasure to others.

M.G.

MATERIALS

Paper

The best paper to use is always good quality Cartridge paper, but less expensive papers can be used if this is not available. Pastel papers or Sugar paper (the grey paper commonly used in schools) are a possible alternative in most cases. As a general rule it will be obvious that thick or stiff papers will produce better results than thinner ones in which there is less support. There are many different types and qualities of paper available, and you will tell best by practical experiment whether a particular paper is suitable for the work you wish to do. If you use a paper and the form sags or begins to collapse as you make it up, the paper is no good and you will have to find something with more strength before you go on with the work.

Cardboard

In some cases thin cardboard can be used for the shapes, but it is only necessary where it is suggested in the text. Cardboard is expensive and for most of the work it would not be a more satisfactory material than paper.

Fixing

In most models it is necessary to fix the paper at some point to hold it in shape. In the diagrams and instructions the suggested fixing points are shown at each stage of the work. Various techniques can be used for making the fixture.

1. An ordinary dressmaker's pin is a cheap and immediately effective method.
2. Paper fasteners — the piercing type which are pushed through and opened flat at the back — are effective but usually require holes pierced through the papers.
3. Staples from an office-type stapling press are a quick and secure method, but in some instances it may be difficult to position the machine at the exact point of fixture. A stapler is a useful part of the equipment, but you are not recommended to buy one until you have reached a standard of work where you think it is essential.
4. Gumming with various types of gum or paste is a possible method of fixing, but this is not recommended since papers have to be held together while gum dries. This tends to waste time and hold up the work. It also makes complications when there are more than two papers to be fixed at one point.

Cutting

All the work suggested can be cut with scissors. Knives may be used but they are not essential. They can be used to score before folding (see Techniques), and they can be used to cut shapes. But this should only be tried where anyone using the knife is old enough to handle it without danger to himself. Paper can be cut with fairly blunt scissors, but a blunt knife is useless.

Total requirements therefore are:
    a pencil
    scissors
    a few pins
    some colouring materials
    and
    a piece of paper.

TECHNIQUES

A technique in a craft is a tried and established method of using the materials. No material in any craft jumps into shape at a look. There must be skill in the hands of the craftsman, so that he can handle the material in the right way. If we examine this skill we find that it begins with an experience of the techniques of the craft.

A sculptor tackling a block of stone uses his tools in the way in which they are best used. He knows what is the best way through his own experience, and through the experience of experts from whom he has been able to learn.

It does not matter how violently he cuts the stone; he will—if he is a real sculptor—make his cuts in the best order and in the right places. He will also treat the stone with respect and consideration—politely in fact—because he knows that a crude treatment can only result in a crude piece of work. A careless blow might cut away stone in the wrong place and thereby ruin part of his design.

If you wanted to become a sculptor you could find a piece of stone and some tools, and you could start work. This is a good, adventurous method of doing something you want to, and it is worthy of praise because it shows determination and spirit. If you kept at it you might ultimately become a very good sculptor.

But if you began by going to a sculptor for advice, he would be able to prevent your getting into certain difficulties in the early stages. He would show you how to hold the tools, which tools to choose, and where to cut the stone. He would also show you where to avoid cutting, and how to develop your work in the most suitable way. In the end you would have a piece of sculpture, rather than the odd shape and pile of chippings which might result from the first method.

The things which he was able to show you would be simple techniques in the craft. These are not rules. They are useful tips, and they would ultimately make your work easier and more satisfying.

Sculpture in paper has a few simple techniques. These basic methods of using the paper, and of raising it from the flat to the state in which it has shape or form, are described and illustrated in the following exercises.

Interested students are recommended to learn and master the techniques by attempting all or some of the exercises, before going on to the later, more complicated models.

SCORING AND FOLDING

Two things occur in a piece of paper when it is folded down the middle:

It is given strength.

It changes visually, usually becoming more interesting.

To understand these two points take any flat piece of paper – a piece about the size of this page will be adequate – and stand it on edge on a flat surface. When you let go it falls down.

Now fold the paper through the middle like a Christmas card and stand it up. In most cases – unless you have a particularly limp piece of paper – it will support itself. It is exactly the same piece of paper but this time, instead of falling flat, it remains standing. It has nothing added to it. The fold has given it strength.

The paper-sculptor uses this technique of folding in various ways to give strength and support in modelling.

To make a neat fold he might also SCORE the paper before folding. In scoring he takes a scissor point or knife blade and cuts into the surface of the paper along the line of the fold. As he does this he makes sure that he does not cut right through the paper anywhere on the score.

After scoring, when he makes the fold, the cut opens slightly along its length. The paper does not resist the fold. And the fold is in exactly the place where he wants it. It is also neater than an unscored fold which might cause the paper to buckle or distort slightly.

Practice in scoring should be done in the first stages on scraps of paper. It will probably be necessary to make a number of attempts before you can judge the amount of pressure which will give you a score and not a cut.

The paper-sculptor also uses the technique to give added visual interest to his work.

After folding and standing a piece of paper you will notice that it now has two surfaces at different angles meeting at the fold. If you look hard enough you will see that these two surfaces – or planes as they are called in sculpture – are different in shade or tone. The plane nearer the window or source of light in the room will be lighter in tone than its partner.

This is a simple example of contrast in which planes, angled together, take on lighter or darker tones. A sculptor makes these contrasts deliberately. He uses the planes – in more complicated arrangements than the example in front of you – in order to define the shape he wants.

Contrast in planes is a visual thing. We see the changes in tone on the surface of the material. And as we see the different planes, a flat surface becomes more interesting and might even begin to tell us something.

As you read this, touch your nose. The side of it makes an angle with the front of your cheek. These two parts of your face are on different planes. The front of your nose and its other side are also different planes.

After touching the planes look in a mirror and try to sort them out visually. You are not looking at your nose. You are looking at surfaces angled together, and visible as different planes because they are slightly different in tone.

The planes you are touching contrast with each other in order to make a shape. This is a shape you know well – it is your nose. The planes then contrast and combine with others to put your nose where it ought to be — on a background of planes which you call your face.

The sculptor works in planes and changes of plane, which he finds in paper by scoring and folding.

Exercises in Straight Scoring and Folding

The exercises in this section may be scored if you are old enough to master the technique. But for younger children the exercises are possible in paper folded without scoring.

Witches

From a piece of paper folded down the middle, cut a triangular shape similar to the one in Fig. 1. You can draw the outline before cutting if it makes you more confident in your work. This is permissible in any of the exercises you attempt.

From the pieces of paper removed when you cut the shape you can cut and attach a broomstick at the side of the witch (Fig. 1a). You can then draw and paint any decoration you like on to the shape.

If you have more paper you can cut other witches of different shapes and sizes. You can have fat ones or tall thin ones, ones with straight hair and ones with curls. On some you can see the legs, on others not.

In this first very simple exercise you can begin to enjoy inventing variations of your own. You can think of people you know and cut witches like them. And you can experiment with colour and pattern, dressing the witches in a variety of clothes. Some can have pattern all over, others can have it at the edges of their clothes. The shapes in the patterns can be different. The faces can be different. You can, if you like, make all your witches gay and smiling. Or you can vary them as people's expressions vary in real life.

If you experiment as you draw the faces you will find out how to make changes in expression. You can make some look alert or surprised, and others can look half-asleep. Some can look angry and some pleased. You can suit yourself.

When you have finished the exercise you can pin some of the witches to your wall — but not flat. Make them stand out a little, with the centre fold giving them form and the support which is necessary to prevent them collapsing over their broomsticks.

Witches — Teaching Note

A diagram drawn on a blackboard as a means of introducing an exercise will have a less uniform result if papers provided for the exercise are cut in different sizes and proportions.

In some later exercises it will be necessary to reproduce diagrams as accurately as possible, but at this stage they need be used only as a guide.

Diagrams shown to a class can be adapted to fit individual shapes, and pupils should be encouraged to draw them large so that there is a minimum waste of paper in the cutting process.

Where possible the technique and its purpose should be explained with the exercise, although it does not have to be understood at the first attempt. Further experience of the technique can be gained from subsequent exercises.

At the completion of any exercise it is desirable that the total work should be displayed in its finished state. The witches can fly on any surface where a simple fixture is possible. They will require pinning or fixing with sticky tape, and should be displayed to show as much of the form as possible.

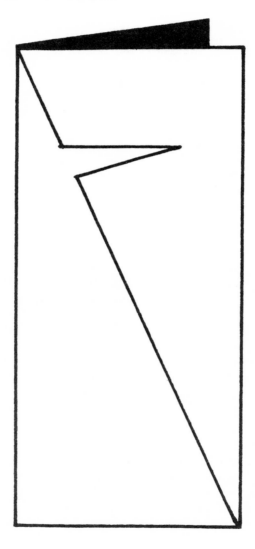

Fig. 1

Fig. 1a

An interesting addition to the exercise might be developed as a background of clouds. These can be cut by the class as individual shapes in thin (kitchen) paper and patterned in tones of blue. With more able pupils a sunset effect might be tried in tones of warm colour.

Roof-tops might also be included in the exercise, with investigation into the shapes and pattern effects of rows of chimneys.

Fig. 1b

Mice

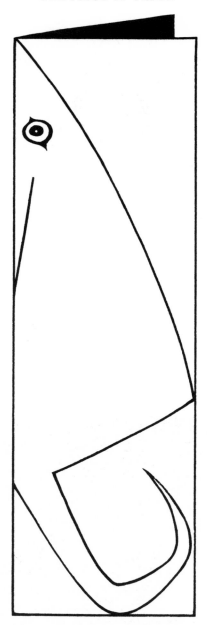

Fig. 2

Other simple shapes can be raised from a flat paper by folding at the centre and cutting the edge.

Simple mouse-shapes can make an interesting decoration for the walls or the ceiling.

In the one suggested in the diagram (Fig. 2) you can make the ears by cutting at an angle into the fold, and cutting along the fold to the base of the ears.

Like the witches, the mice can be long and thin or short and fat, and there is no limit to the type of decoration you can use.

In these, and other animal shapes which you will make as you work through the exercises, you should try to make the eyes as emphatic as possible. The most effective type of eye has a clearly defined white eyeball with a dark pupil at its centre.

If you cut the mice with tails you can make them interesting, and can avoid an unnecessary waste of paper, by turning the tail in a curve towards the body.

You can also add feet when cutting the mice. Some of those illustrated in the photograph (2a) have feet included, but this type of extra is not essential. In this work it is desirable to keep the finished product as simple and direct as possible. Fussy and unnecessary details which complicate the work can make the shapes unnecessarily difficult. The simple form of the models will not be clear, especially when they are mounted or displayed so that they must be seen from a distance.

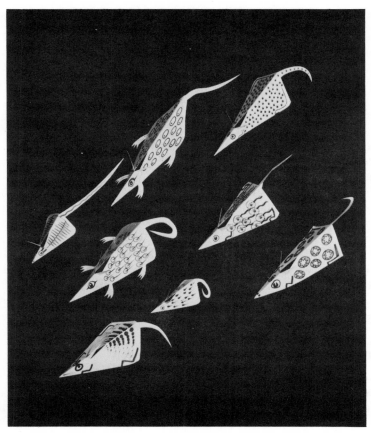

Fig. 2a

Mice – Teaching Note

Paper prepared for the mice can again be in different proportions so that the exercise presents slightly different problems throughout the class. With a large class it is clearly impossible to prepare a different size for each member of the class, but three or four sizes should be enough to start with. Pupils will produce further variations as they cut the mice to their own shape.

Various suitable backgrounds can be prepared to go with the mice.

Sacks of flour can be cut from brown wrapping paper, or even from sheets of newspaper, and can be stuck to the background in a pile.

Ears of corn can be cut from kitchen paper. These should be as large and bold as possible, and might in themselves be simple exercises in pattern.

When the mice are mounted the form should be raised as much as possible. They can be mounted to run over any suitable surface – including the ceiling, which in some classrooms can be a very valuable area for displaying work.

Animals with an Ark

Some people who try to work creatively in a craft are able to make only very slow progress because they are timid. They are frightened of spoiling their work, and, because they never take a risk, they often find it difficult to make their work exciting.

It is true that confidence grows with practice and developing ability, but exciting and satisfying work is possible in the early stages of a craft if bold steps can be taken in the treatment of the material.

In this exercise take a piece of paper up to half Imperial size. Choose an animal and draw its body on the paper – large and without a head (Fig. 3). Cut this shape out and then cut the remaining paper into two pieces. Fold each of them down the middle, and make them both into heads for the animal.

Since this is an exercise in the technique of raising form by folding, the heads should be drawn and cut full-face, the fold being down the centre from forehead to nose. They do not have to be exactly the same size or shape.

After cutting the three shapes, and after decorating them with suitable pattern, you can mount the body flat on the wall. The two heads can be added – with raised form – to suggest one animal peering from behind the other.

As further exercises you can, if you like, make a series of animals. These can be mounted, as in the photograph (Fig. 3a), following one another into an ark. The ark, which should be a simple shape, can also be given form by folding at the centre.

Animals with an Ark – Teaching Note

This exercise can be done in grey sugar paper which can be prepared in various shapes. Time might profitably be spent in the introductory stage in listing some of the large variety of animals suitable for the exercise. Time might also be spent in making sure that the body shapes are drawn as simple and bold statements – not as academic studies.

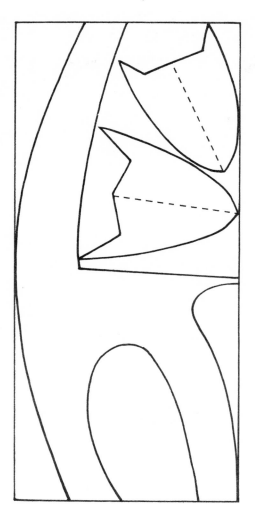

Fig. 3

If the exercise is attempted as a class project preliminary organisation must take in the direction in which the animals are drawn. This must depend on the position of the Ark in the final displayed project, and the mounting space for the animals. This is a minor point. But if the animals are all walking to the left, it will not be possible to mount the Ark in the middle of the display.

Many of the exercises suggested can be attempted with their backgrounds as class projects, and in each of them a little simple organisation will be necessary in the early stages. If the project is adequately planned, the classroom work will go smoothly, and the major amount of time will be spent by the pupils in the preparation and decorative treatment of their own individual contributions.

Fig. 3a

Standing Figures

Since the technique of scoring and folding gives visual interest and support, it can be practised on exercises which can stand as well as on those suitable for mounting.

For these exercises it will be necessary to use very stiff paper (best quality cartridge) or thin cardboard.

The most profitable source of ideas for these exercises is in the people around you.

A strip of card—any size up to 20 inches high by about 8 inches wide—folded down the middle, can be cut to a simple shape and decorated to represent a type of person. If possible a score should be made before folding, although this is only for neatness—it is not essential.

In cutting the figure it is necessary to keep a simple shape. Thin legs and small feet are obviously not possible since the model is intended to stand. But even without these the shapes can be made interesting and amusing.

The most successful results will be those in which you make the right choice of subject. An ordinary type of man in a blue suit will be less striking than a figure in uniform—a soldier or a high dignitary in splendid robes of office. Circus figures are particularly suitable for this exercise because they are colourful as well as interesting in shape. Among these you can find clowns—particularly suitable with their baggy shapeless trousers—and animals sitting on highly decorated boxes.

Figures from film and television will sometimes make interesting exercises — cowboys and Red Indians with splendid head-dresses standing by their decorated wigwams. The wigwams can be made in the same way with a fold at the middle.

There are other opportunities with figures from books. Figures from history are particularly suitable: knights and warriors, or kings and queens in period costume. These and many other different types of people, both from history and from the present day, can be used.

You will learn as you do the exercises, and by keeping your shapes very simple you will begin to develop an appreciation for the style of work best suited to this craft. Complicated and difficult cutting will probably be less effective than the simpler shapes which say what they have to without unnecessary fuss.

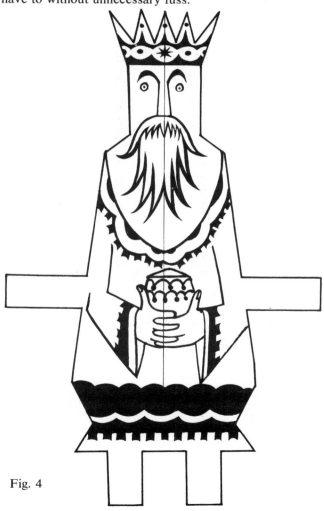

Fig. 4

Where you want to display figures for any length of time you can make sure that they remain folded and in position by incorporating RETURNS. These are illustrated in the diagram of a king (Fig. 4).

Returns in paper sculpture are flaps included in the model at points where they can be used to make a fixture. In the diagram the king is shown with flaps at the sides and on the bottom edge. When the figure is required to stand, the flaps at the sides can be fixed together at the back of the model (Fig. 4a). This will hold the angle of the planes in a permanently fixed position, and will prevent the cardboard from returning to a flat shape.

The flaps on the bottom edge will overlap when you make the fold. It will then be possible to pin the model through these flaps in a secure position at the rear. This method of fixing is useful when models are incorporated into a display which is to be left in position for any length of time.

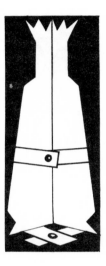

Fig. 4a

Standing Figure Projects

Figure exercises can be made more interesting by incorporating them into planned projects. A circus has interesting possibilities, or the characters in a play. A series of figures might show the history of uniform in the army, or a history of costume and changing fashions.

A very suitable project is the Christmas nativity scene (see Fig. 4b). This should be made as large as possible within the limits of the space which is available for its display. It can include:

The kings similar to the one illustrated. These should be decorated with rich colour and pattern, and with expensive-looking ornament.

The shepherds can be simpler, with bold patterns and stripes in plain colours.

The figure of Joseph can be similar to the shepherds. But it should be cut rather taller than the Mary figure which, being shorter, can be made to appear in a sitting position with folds painted on the skirt.

The figure of Mary can be painted holding the infant Jesus, or a separate crib can be cut and folded to stand in front of her.

Fig. 4b

Animals for the stable can be made with the same technique as the figures. A simple method is illustrated in Figures 5 and 5a. The head and ears at the top must be turned down to the front of the body after cutting. The direction of the fold on the head is then reversed by folding the whole shape again like a Christmas card.

Since a shape like this will not stand if it is cut with thin animal-like legs, the lower part of the animal can be cut and painted to suggest a stall in front of—and hiding—most of the body.

The diagram shows a suggested shape for a donkey. If it is cut double, the sides will be identical and it will have two tails when it is opened. One of these must, of course, be cut away.

The donkey can be made to look more like a cow by cutting the ears smaller, and by including horns. On the diagram these should be positioned immediately below the ears, and should be pointing downwards. After cutting and folding they will point upwards between the ears.

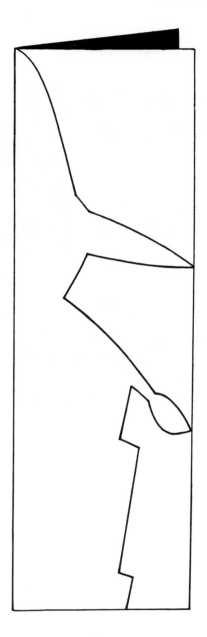

Fig. 5

Fig. 5a

A suitable background for the nativity scene can be prepared in the same way as the rest of the model. A number of pieces of card, cut with a suggestion of a sloping roof and with windows, can be painted to represent the rough walls of the stable. If these are set overlapping each other behind the figure groups the idea of a stable interior will be suggested in the project, and the display will be held together (see Fig. 4b).

Nativity – Teaching Note

The project suggested in this exercise can be used as a class opportunity for the involvement of every member. Practical work in Art and Craft is not always satisfactory in schools when only the most successful results can be displayed. There are times when even the least capable pupil can be allowed to make a slight but real contribution to work intended for public display.

In a project like the one suggested, an 'arranged' allocation of the individual parts is obviously necessary. Some parts are easier than others. The animals and the stable backgrounds require less skill than the figures, and if they are made rather ineptly in some cases, they can be easily hidden somewhere in the background.

If cardboard in prepared sizes is available for the project the problem of an erratic scale – with giants and midgets – will not arise. To this end, pupils should be encouraged to plan their work so that a minimum amount of card has to be cut away to establish the shape.

Background shapes, animals, walls and even unidentified figures can be included in the project in any number, so that every class member can be involved in the work.

A further background for the standing project can be prepared on frieze paper – or alternatively on cartridge paper in rolls, ceiling paper or on the back of an unwanted roll of wallpaper.

This can be painted with a hot sky and a sandy ground, and with buildings and trees. Or it can be effectively decorated with stuck tissue-paper.

A sky in black tissue-paper, with a bottom edge torn unevenly and stuck on a yellow ground, will make an interesting background for cut paper buildings.

These can be prepared at the same time as the crib scene, and can involve – under supervision – the less able pupils. The finished background can be pinned behind the cut-out shapes to complete the display.

CURVING THE SCORE

The technique of scoring and folding can be further developed in paper sculpture by the introduction of curves.

If you cut two flat shapes, for example two simple fish, you can score them without using a ruler or straight edge. The first score, made by holding the knife like a pen, should be made as a gentle curve. In the second example the curve can be slightly more elaborate (Figs. 6 and 6a).

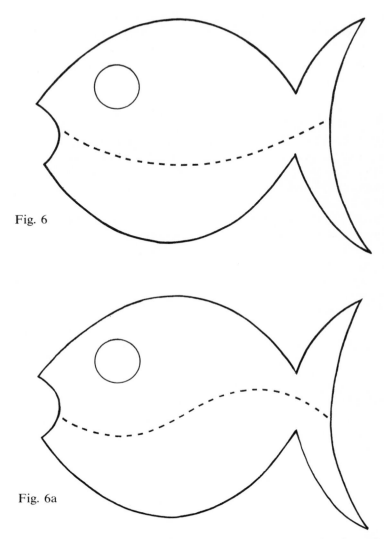

Fig. 6

Fig. 6a

After scoring, form can be raised by folding the shapes gently along the scores. It will be different in the two examples suggested because every variation in the curve of a score produces a different form. When raising the form you should try to find it on the score, and should avoid buckling the paper into any shape which is not the result of the score.

You can develop an interesting exercise by cutting other fish in different shapes and sizes, and raising them to interesting forms. They can be decorated and mounted to make an interesting wall display.

If you find it difficult to make interesting variations in the shapes and patterns of the fish you can look at illustrations in reference books. It is not necessary — nor is it very helpful — to copy the illustrations, but they can be used as ideas for the development of your own work. If you need suggestions and ideas at any stage of your work, it is quite permissible to turn to books — or to museums and other sources of reference.

Fig. 6b

Fish — Teaching Note

Fish shapes, cut flat and given form on a fold, will be useful supplements to a number of later exercises in the book.

In exercises with a curved score, experiments can be attempted with more able pupils, but some of the work can be done by younger children. They can use a straight fold to give the shapes form.

As in other exercises the fish shapes should be cut from a variety of papers, and they should be cut with a minimum waste at the edges.

Drawn outlines will be necessary in some cases before cutting.

Caterpillars

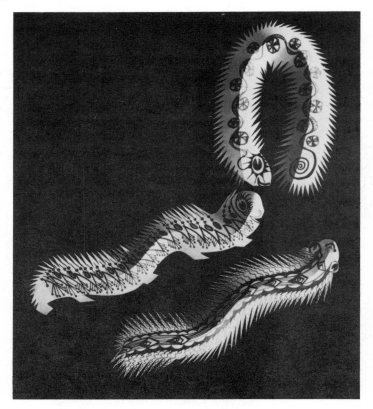

Fig. 7

When you are able to make a simple curved score you can develop further ability in the technique by trying more ambitious exercises.

Caterpillar shapes will provide good opportunities for experiments with curved scores on larger pieces of paper (see photograph 7). The caterpillars can be made to wriggle, or they can be bent at the middle. For further effect the edges can be cut in spiky patterns, and the caterpillars can be mounted on large patterned leaves.

If you look in your garden or in a public park you will find leaves in many different shapes and in many different tones of colour. This might help you to make the background interesting. You should try mixing some of the different tones instead of using the same colour on all the leaves.

For other exercises in curving the score you could make a decoration with any shape which has a curved tail. A row of cats on a wall can have a variety of tails. Or you could make squirrels and birds in a wood. There are many opportunities for lively and interesting exercises as you practise the techniques.

THE CUT TO THE CENTRE

Another method used by paper sculptors to raise form is to cut into the paper and overlap the edges of the cut. If you draw and cut out a circle on paper the result is a flat disc. If you cut from the edge to the centre of the disc — or as near to the centre as you can judge — you will find it possible to overlap the sides of the cut so that the disc becomes a cone. The paper now has a form which can be raised or made flatter by changing the amount of overlap.

The raised form can be retained in the paper by fixing the overlap in the position required. It can be pinned, stapled or gummed, but if gum is used the overlap must be held in position with a paper clip until the gum has dried.

A number of these shapes made as an exercise can be decorated and mounted like balloons. You can fix cottons from them to the figure of the balloon seller (Fig. 8) if it is not possible to draw strings on the wall.

This is a simple technique requiring very little skill. When you can understand it you can go on to exercises in which you begin to combine the techniques.

Fig. 8

Fireworks

The type of disc suggested in the previous exercise can be cut at its edges like a whirling firework, and can be patterned to add to the effect (see the photograph, 8a).

A bonfire can be suggested with simple flame shapes which can be given form by scoring and folding. These can be patterned and mounted round a guy, and the fireworks added for effect.

Fig. 8a

Fireworks – Teaching Note

It is not necessary to rush this type of exercise in order to complete it in one lesson. The flames can be an exercise in themselves, each member of the class making one the height of an Imperial sheet. The fireworks can be made in various sizes. To make the circles for these, pupils can draw round convenient objects.

The intention of the exercise is not to make pupils cut precise circles. Its main object is to provide opportunity for the manipulation of colour and pattern on a shape more interesting to a child than the familiar rectangle.

Display of this exercise will be made more effective by the use of a black background. A concentration of fireworks near the bonfire can be further enhanced by pinning one or two of them in different parts of the room, as though they have exploded away from the main mass.

For another classroom exercise pupils could cut snails, and raise form in the side of the shells. In this case, on the paper provided they might first draw a large arch from the bottom corners to the middle of the top edge. This can be cut out and decorated, and the snail's head and tail made from the off-cuts. After fixing and patterning, form can be raised in the shell by cutting in from the edge.

A simple exercise for a few children can be developed with a flat cut-out clown juggling with decorated shapes. The shapes can again be simple circles cut to the centre.

Interesting hanging shapes can be developed by joining cones together in pairs. These can be made as Christmas decorations. They can be effective and amusing with pattern on one side and a face on the other. The cones pin together easily, and are light enough to be hung from strings stretched across the room.

Faces and Portraits

Most of you will have drawn and painted a portrait, either at home if you are interested or in one of your art lessons.

Form raised by cutting into a shape can produce amusing results in portrait work.

To try this take a piece of paper as large as you can get — up to Imperial size — and tear it into two equal pieces.

On one of the two pieces draw a portrait head and shoulders — full-face, that is looking towards you, as you see your own face when you look straight at a mirror.

Draw the same portrait on the second piece. It does not have to be exactly the same. This would be very difficult and would be a case for very serious study. But without making it too much of a burden you should try to get both drawings as nearly alike as possible.

After making the second drawing you can cut round the outline of the face and can remove it from the background. By making a cut in the bottom of the chin — two or three inches into the face — you can give the shape form by overlapping. If you fix the form you can then pin the face in position on the first drawing.

It will probably be necessary to pin the face to the background at the top of the head and at the chin. With the two pieces joined together and painted as one picture you will have an amusing and unusual type of portrait, with the face apparently growing out of the picture.

If you do this exercise you should be able to make a mask. And one mask — the first you make—can lead to another, until you have your own wardrobe of masks. You might even make a totem-pole of masks pinned above each other on the wall. You can vary the shapes by having form at the top as well as at the bottom of the masks. But until you have done many more exercises you should still keep your shapes very simple.

Faces and Portraits – Teaching Note

The raised portrait can be a lively class exercise in itself. But it can also be developed in various interesting ways.

Instead of individual portraits the class can make a group of people. These can be life-size with the bodies cut flat and the faces raised. At Christmas the group can be composed of clowns or angels, but at any other time of the year any crowd of people will serve as a point of departure for the exercise. A crowd at a bus-stop, or at a lunch counter—seen from behind the counter through the sandwiches and cakes, or a crowd posing at a wedding.

Class exercises developed from the simple techniques go well when they incorporate as many stimulating opportunities as possible. This is often best done by developing the original exercise through a series of lessons in each of which there is an opportunity for practical work.

The following example (Fig. 9) is included as a guide to illustrate the possible development of a simple exercise when it is exploited with some imagination. The exercise in this case is still that of raising form on a cut.

First Lesson

Half Imperial kitchen or some other thin paper—cut longways 30×11 inches.

Off-cuts of sugar or cartridge paper left over from previous lessons.

The exercise should begin with pupils drawing a roof with chimneys at the top of the paper. This shape should be interesting but not too complicated, since it has to be cut out.

After the roof has been cut, a large window should be drawn on the house, and treated like the portrait in the previous exercise. It can be given an occupant with a raised face—someone looking through the window.

The raised part of the figure can be made from scraps and pinned to the background. When the figure has been painted the rest of the house can be decorated.

Left alone, a number of children in any class would continue the exercise from this point by painting the house brown or some other dark colour. Some of the results would please neither the children nor their teachers. The failures in a class tend to be forgotten in the light of the more successful work done by the more able pupils in a group.

A controlled exercise can often help the child who finds it persistently difficult to make his work as attractive as that of others. The control is a measure of assistance at the beginning of the work.

In the present exercise large rectangles and squares drawn on the house can be painted in bright colours, or—with more able children—in tones of one colour. This is a simple type of decorative rather than realistic treatment, and is only one of a variety of different styles to which children can be introduced.

The value of these styles of work lies in the new and varied experiences which they provide for the pupils.

A house painted in brown and black by a child makes an end result which is a visual experience. Another house painted by the same child in large rectangles of bright colour results in a different visual experience. The many ways of painting a house with a decorative treatment cannot be listed, because the potential variations in tone and shape are so numerous. Any way which can be discovered and introduced to a class may be valuable in the opportunity it provides for a new visual experience.

After pupils have painted the squares and rectangles suggested in this exercise, they can complete the houses as they like — with further colour and pattern.

This exercise can be further developed in other lessons, using the completed ones as a reasonable point of departure for the next.

Fig. 9

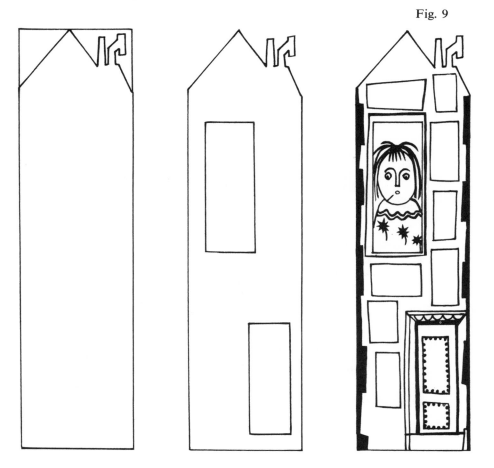

Fig. 10

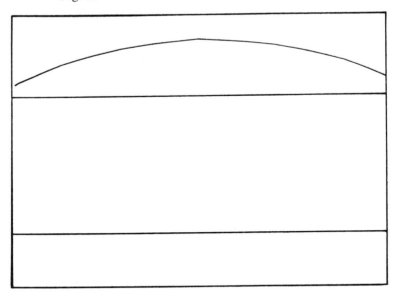

Fig. 10a

Second Lesson

One sheet of sugar paper Imperial size. If this is too large for use in an overcrowded room, the exercise can be scaled down to a suitable size.

The exercise should begin with pupils painting or drawing freely on their papers the three lines indicated in Fig. 10—a shallow arch and two parallel lines.

The portion above the arch can be painted white, with blue lines indicating brickwork.

A number of faces with raised form can be placed between the parallel lines, and painted into the background to represent people travelling in an underground train (Fig. 10a).

To add variety to the exercise pupils should be encouraged to develop the people as individuals. Further suggestions of form can be introduced to help the picture.

A figure reading a newspaper can, for example, be holding a piece cut from a real newspaper. This can be pinned to the background and can have form on a straight fold. Hands can be painted on so that the figure appears to be holding the paper.

Other figures can carry different cut-outs. Flowers can be added to one, or a musical instrument—even an animal; anything, in fact, which the children can think of and translate into simple visual terms.

The exercises can be completed by adding pattern and colour where possible, and by painting wheels in the lower section against a black background. When they are pinned up in a row the end results will suggest a train travelling under the houses. The bricked white areas above the arches will act as a key holding the work together, and making the component parts—whether they are good or bad—into one whole thing.

This is not a serious exercise. Nor is it intended to have any deep significance.

It is the type of exercise which can be fun for pupils involved in it. They can learn as they work, and they can all contribute to the end product.

Many other similar exercises are possible. The cross-section of a building, upstairs and down, with different types of people. A multiple store, with the side removed in the same way, like a doll's house, to show different departments. A restaurant on various floors, with a roof garden with striped umbrellas—and with kitchens in the cellars.

In this and other exercises the work might occupy a single lesson, or it might be allowed to develop through a number of lessons.

In either case the content of the lessons, and the methods of treating the subjects, should be lively enough to prevent the necessary practice of techniques from becoming a dull business.

CURLING

A flat piece of paper has the same tension on both sides. If you upset the tension on one of the sides the paper will curl.

You can demonstrate this for yourself by taking a strip of paper—about an inch wide and twelve to eighteen inches long. Holding the end of it in one hand, you should scrape a knife or scissor blade along the under-side of it in one movement—starting from the point where you are holding the strip. The edge of the blade should travel evenly along the length of the strip, and should be supported by the thumb at the top, so that the paper passes in a direct movement between the edge of the blade and the thumb.

When the blade leaves the free end of the paper, the even tension has been disturbed and the strip should spring into a tight curl. It can be made tighter or looser by varying the pressure between blade and thumb, but this must be practised.

It is not a difficult technique, and anyone attempting it should be able to get the pressure and the motion right after a few attempts. On some of the earlier attempts the paper will probably break at the point where it is held. But this is usual, and the pressure can be corrected with practice.

Practice in the technique can be developed into amusing exercises.

The witches made in an earlier exercise can have hair included. This will involve a little more complicated cutting, but the strips which are to be curled can be kept very simple.

These strips will have to be quite thin, and must be held at the point where they join the main shape as each one is curled. If they are too thin and you find that you are tearing them from the shape you should attempt an exercise in which the strips are less fragile.

Exercise in the technique might be easier with hair on faces cut from larger paper. These can be quite large masks with much thicker strips for hair, and they can be made into interesting exercises by giving them folded or overlapped form (see Fig. 11).

A group of faces made in this way could provide an interesting decoration for a party. You could model each of your guests. The results might not be very successful as likenesses, but they might make your guests laugh—which is what you want at a party.

You could also make a group of faces into another totem-pole, in which case it would not be necessary to pattern them on people you know.

Curling—Teaching Note

This is a simple technique which is best practised in the bold treatment of large shapes. Heads cut from the largest paper available make a very suitable exercise, and can be highly decorative when mounted.

Totem-poles are useful at this stage in the development of the work, and can also be introduced as exercises in the techniques already described.

Forms for the totem-poles can be made in sugar paper with a simple background shape and an added nose. They can be made in a free range of colours or they can be used as controlled exercises in special colour experiences.

A class might make two quite different totem-poles. In one of them the forms could be painted in bold stripes of black and white with one other colour. The visual effect of this might be compared with that of the second totem-pole painted by the class without direction.

The controlled exercise might not be an improvement on the other. It is not intended as such. It is an experience which will augment the normal work and add a little to the visual education of those pupils involved in the exercises.

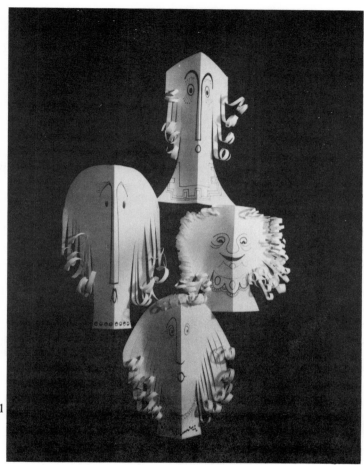

Fig. 11

FORMS FROM ONE PIECE OF PAPER

If you have experimented with the techniques already described you should be ready to manipulate paper into a variety of shapes.

It will probably not be easy to devise shapes of your own until you are fairly experienced. But you should begin to have an idea of a few of the possible shapes which are hidden in any piece of paper.

You should also begin to have a feeling for the material, and should be developing the gentle but firm touch which is necessary in paper sculpture.

The shapes which follow can be found in a single piece of paper. They are practical exercises intended to help and amuse you, and to give you confidence in the craft of folding and cutting—and raising form in paper.

If you are able to go on later to shapes of your own it will probably be because you have mastered the necessary techniques, and have seen and appreciated some of the ways in which form can be raised from a flat piece of paper.

The shapes suggested are not serious attempts to create photographic likenesses. Nor do they reproduce with accuracy every detail of the form they represent.

They are exercises in a light-hearted craft, and any work undertaken on them should be enjoyed—both in making the shapes and in their subsequent decoration.

Some care is necessary in the work. But the main thing is to enjoy it. If you are aware of this and have practised the techniques, you are ready to go on to the next exercise.

LIZARD

Size: Quarter Imperial (15 × 11 inches)

Drawing the Diagram (Fig. 12)

In all the exercises in which the model can be cut with the paper doubled, the fold is shown as the left side of the diagram. You can check that you are drawing the diagram correctly by using the shaded portion at the top, which points in each case to the main fold in the paper.

By studying the diagram carefully before drawing you may in each case be able to pick out important or helpful points. You may also begin to understand the diagram and see a connection between the flat shape and the raised form.

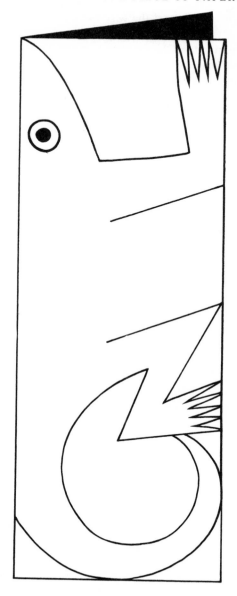

Fig. 12

In the present example (Fig. 12) the following points may be helpful:
The front of the lizard is at the top of the diagram.
The front leg touches the top of the paper.
The back leg touches the right side of the diagram at approximately half way.
The tail curves round from the folded side – which is the spine of the lizard – and

touches the back leg. This is to avoid the waste of paper which would result from a long straight tail.

When you begin to understand the diagram you can draw it on your own paper. Some rubbing-out or alteration may be necessary, but when you are satisfied that it bears a reasonable resemblance to the illustration you can cut the shape.

Since this is done with the paper doubled you will have a shape with two tails.

Raising the Form

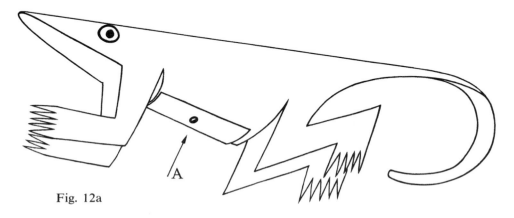

Fig. 12a

Continue the line of one of the tails to the body and cut it away.

The flaps between the front and back legs must be turned under the body to make a cylinder. This must be fixed under the belly (A in Fig. 12a).

There is no lower jaw in the finished shape. This omission may worry you as you make the model. But after fixing the belly you should paint in the eyes, and fix the shape to a wall.

The lizard is intended to appear as though it is crawling on the wall, and is designed to be seen from this angle — that is, looking directly at its back.

In this case the model does not need an under-jaw, which would be an unnecessary complication in the earlier stages. When you look at your watch you do not turn it over and examine the back. You take it for granted that the back is there. The same can apply to the lizard. The lower jaw is not visible, therefore you can assume that it is there.

It is often possible in art to leave out details and to get away with it. In some instances the omission of details will actually improve the quality of the work. This is particularly so when a work has to make a simple impact, and when it must appeal visually without requiring a great deal of thought and speculation.

In the type of paper sculpture suggested in this book we are concerned with simple shapes which can be displayed as decorative features after they are made. They do not have to be correct in detail because they are intended to be more deccrative than realistic.

As decorations they will be seen from a distance, and work on unnecessary details will be wasted.

The underside of the lizard is included—although like the jaw most of it would be invisible after mounting—in order to give the shape more form than it would have with a simple fold.

The lizard is in fact a development on the mouse suggested in an earlier exercise. If you understand this development it might be possible for you to devise further shapes of your own in the style of the lizard. Any creature which has four legs and which crawls might be a possible subject for experiment.

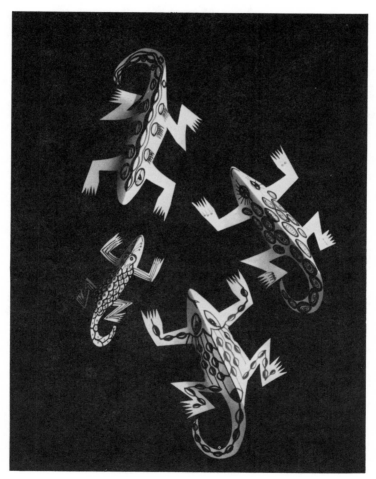

Fig. 12b

Lizard — Teaching Note

Like any of the examples suggested the lizard can be used as a background shape for an exercise in colour and pattern. Treating an animal shape with pattern might be more interesting to pupils than working on a familiar rectangle.

After decoration the shapes can be mounted on any suitable surface with pins or with sticky tape, or they can be displayed on a prepared background.

Preparation of the background can be planned and carried out as an additional class exercise. Various methods are possible.

Half Imperial paper — cut longways 30×11 inches — can be prepared by each member of the class and mounted side by side to make a long frieze shape.

Odd shapes, triangles and irregularly cut pieces which have no particular bottom or top, can be prepared and built up like a patchwork to fill a particular area.

A suitable background for the lizards might be an exercise in very hot colour and pattern. Each pupil can treat his own part of the background all over in hot sandy colours. On top of this, drawing freely with a brush, he can add large pebble shapes, which can themselves be patterned — either in additional colour or in black and white.

Methods of treating the pebbles might be stimulated where possible by allowing pupils to handle and examine actual pebbles collected from the shore.

Other possible backgrounds might be developed in different ways. A plain coloured ground patterned all over with lizard-like footprints will provide a different visual experience. A simple rock face can be developed with patterns of fissures and cracks. Any exercise is valuable if it provides an opportunity for practical experiment with colour and pattern, and if it results in an end product which is a new visual experience for the pupils concerned.

FLY OR BUMBLE-BEE

Size: Quarter Imperial

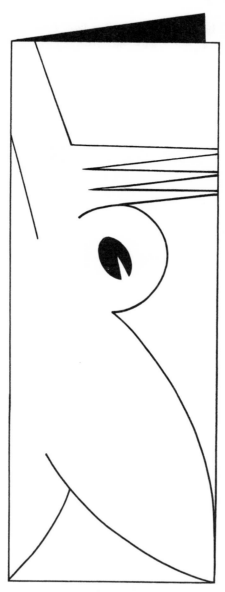

Fig. 13

Drawing the Diagram (Fig. 13)

The round shape is the eye. The bottom of this shape is approximately the centre point of the rectangle. Other parts of the diagram can be related to this point.

The line on the left side of the diagram indicates a cut into the fold. It does not quite reach the middle of the eye.

The horizontal lines above the eye are intended to represent simple legs.

Below the eye, the larger shape with the curved sides is the wing. The smaller curved shape at the bottom is the body with the fold through its centre.

Raising the Form

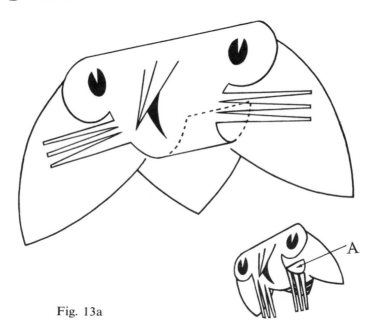

Fig. 13a

After cutting, open the shape out flat.

To raise the lizard in the previous exercise you turned the sides down and made a cylinder along part of the length of the form. In this exercise it is necessary to make the cylinder across the form — by turning the top down and into the back. This can be seen more clearly in Fig. 13a, where the dotted line indicates the part of the paper on the inside of the cylinder. A single fixture is made at this point (A), where the inner paper of the cylinder must be fixed to the back of the shape.

As the shape is bent into a cylinder the pointed section will stick out where the cut was made in the fold. This makes a suitable indication of a nose in front of the eyes.

After the cylinder has been fixed, the legs will stick out sideways. They must be bent downwards as in the photograph (13b).

This shape is easy to raise from the flat, and if a pin is used to make the fixture at (A) the model can be opened flat to make painting easier. It can be painted and patterned as a fly in tones of blue and green. Or it can be made like a bumble-bee with yellow and black stripes.

Finished shapes can be pinned to the wall, or they can be hung freely on thin cottons.

For the best visual effect the shapes should be treated on both sides with pattern and colour, since parts of both sides are visible in the finished model.

Fig. 13b

Fly or Bumble-Bee – Teaching Note

A background is not necessary if the flies are to be hung. But if they are to be mounted on a wall various subjects can be suitable for further class exercises.

Individual pieces of paper can be cut to represent dustbins and can be mounted in a row — with a decorative rather than a sordid treatment.

Smaller papers can be made into the shapes of jars of jam or preserves, which offer interesting possibilities for colour and pattern.

If you are interested in filling a large wall space somewhere in the school, the area might be prepared to suggest a patterned tablecloth — with squares of painted kitchen paper stuck in place. Kitchen paper — or some other equally thin substitute — sticks well to a wall when powder paste is used, and can be easily removed later by soaking.

After preparing the wall to suggest a tablecloth, pupils can cut large circles of kitchen paper and decorate them as plates. Various patterned and colourful foodstuffs can be cut or painted on the plates. These will make an amusing background for the flies. This must be a gay decoration — a light-hearted opportunity for interesting shapes with colour and pattern. It is not intended to be a grisly warning on the dangers of contaminated food.

If the shapes are painted with stripes to look more like bumble-bees, a background of hives in an orchard can be worked out with individual contributions from each member of the class. A more colourful exercise might be developed in the preparation of a large expanse of flowers for the bees to work on. These can be cut individually as large as possible, and can be coloured and patterned before being mounted.

A background is of course not essential to this or to any of the exercises. The shapes can be mounted against a plain wall. They should be decorative and attractive enough in themselves, but a suitable background can often be combined with work on the shape to make an interesting series of lessons.

SEAGULL

Size: Quarter Imperial, but can be made effectively larger—up to half Imperial.

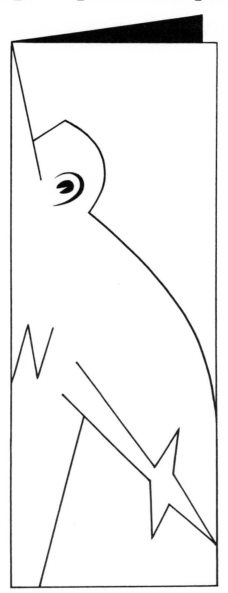

Fig. 14

Drawing the Diagram (Fig. 14)

The Z-shaped cut into the fold is slightly below the middle of the height.

The thin pointed shape at the top of the diagram is the beak.

Reading downwards on the right from this you have the head with the eye, the wing and the leg.

The points at the bottom of the leg are included to suggest a simple foot-shape.

Raising the Form

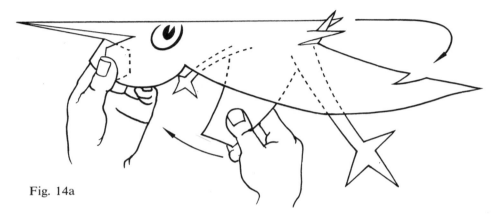

Fig. 14a

Open the shape out flat after cutting.

Raise form in the head by overlapping the front edges under the beak.

Hold these edges together in one hand—as shown in Fig. 14a—and pull the back of the shape down and under to meet the overlapping flaps at the front.

It should now be possible to hold the three pieces of paper at the same point. These three—the two sides of the head and the front of the belly—must be secured with one fixture (A in Fig. 14b).

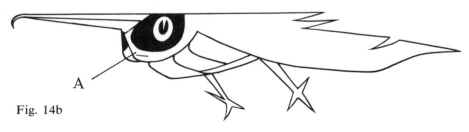

A

Fig. 14b

You can now fold the legs down from the sides of the wings into a reasonably natural position.

The pointed end of the beak can be curled slightly downwards to give the seagull a suitably greedy look.

When you paint the shape it will be effective to make the beak and legs orange or bright yellow. The rest of the seagull can be treated in any way which appeals to you.

Your decoration on this or any of the models can be applied to the surface with paint or crayon, or if you are able to use a sharp knife, by cutting into the surface to make patterns. This is an alternative method to painting. You can see it, and the type of visual effect it makes, on some of the models in the photographs. It is an interesting departure from the usual methods of decoration, and students who are able to use sharp knives may like to explore some of its possibilities in their work. But this should be in addition to the exercises in colour and pattern which can be developed through work with the models.

The seagull shapes are good exercises for developing pattern in one colour. If they are made in white cartridge paper, with orange or yellow beaks and heads, they might be more effectively patterned in tones of blue than in mixed colours. A black area round the eyes will help to suggest the head as a unit although it is, in fact, a single form with the body.

Fig. 14c

The gulls can be hung from any point on the shape, and a group of them will make an effective decoration—either for fun or for a party. Hung in different ways—nose-diving, flying upwards, sideways or the wrong way up, they will give the appearance of gulls tumbling about in the air as they do in real life.

Gulls — Teaching Note

It is very often a valuable experience for children to work in a limited colour range. With one colour—and black and white—they can investigate variations in lighter or darker tones. This is good practice for later work in wider ranges of colour, and might be introduced where the exercise is suitable.

The gulls tend to be more effective for single colour work, since a variety of colours on the shape tends to detract from the simple impact of the final form.

Where the gulls are to be hung in a room they might be linked as a display with some of the fish shapes and backgrounds which are suggested in later exercises.

SEAHORSE

Size: Half Imperial (22 × 15 inches) or smaller

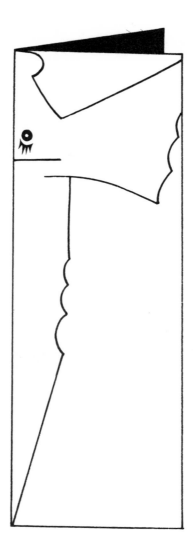

Fig. 15

Drawing the Diagram (Fig. 15)

In this shape very exact proportions are not as important as they are in some others. The shape should have a body about three times as long as the head.

Cut decorations in the body—like the curves shown—are not essential in the diagram stage. To simplify the diagram they can be left out, and introduced after the shape is made up.

The horizontal cut into the fold is parallel along part of its length with a cut from the other side. The paper between these two cuts will hold the head to the body.

Raising the Form

Keep the model folded down the centre line, and hold it in one hand below the horizontal cuts.

Fold the head forwards and down over the body as in Fig. 15a. The rear part of the head and the projection at its back will cover part of the body.

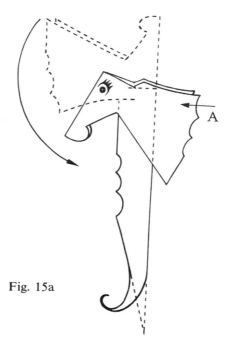

Fig. 15a

When you fold the head down, the horizontal cuts will act as a hinge between the body and the head. This hinge should be pinched together between the fingers when the head is in position.

A permanent fixture is necessary at the back of the head (A).

After patterning, the bottom of the tail can be curled slightly upwards to complete the shape.

The seahorses can be pinned to a background, or they can be strung with cottons and allowed to hang freely.

By adjusting the diagram you can make them thicker or thinner to your own preference. But in any change of proportion the horizontal cuts must overlap sufficiently to act as a hinge between the head and body.

The models should be coloured on both sides.

Fig. 15b

Sea Horses – Teaching Note

As a class exercise this is a useful vehicle for work in pattern, but it can be rather wasteful with paper.

In order to avoid this the large areas of paper cut away at the sides of the body should be kept for use in other exercises. They might in this instance be made into smaller sea-horses, or they might be kept for later development as smaller examples of some of the exercises to be introduced to the class.

Suitable backgrounds are suggested in the teaching notes in later exercises with fish shapes. The seahorse can be combined with these into class projects.

It can also be undertaken as an exercise in its own right, with the finished works in various sizes mounted on an untreated wall or background.

This may be because in reality the seahorse is a creature with a stiff and formal air, and the shape lends itself to a precise type of mounting and display.

OWL

Size: Half Imperial or smaller

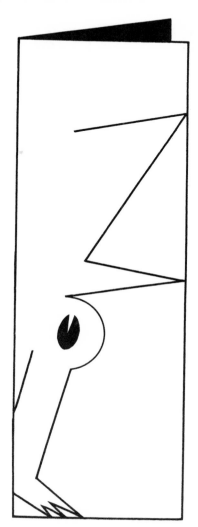

Fig. 16

Drawing the Diagram (Fig. 16)

The pointed shape at the top of the eye touches the side halfway down its length.

The beak-shape requires a single cut into the fold.

The wing is made with a simple V-cut into the upper part of the shape at the side opposite the fold.

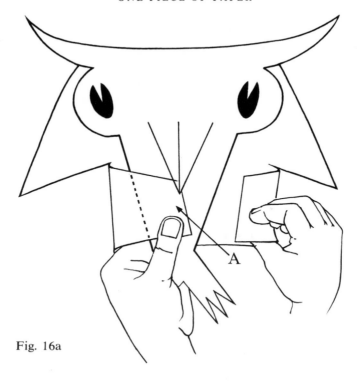

Fig. 16a

Raising the Form

The shape must be opened flat after cutting.

The paper above the eyes must be folded backwards and down behind the front of the model, leaving the horizontal pointed shapes at the top.

The lower portions at the back beneath the wings can be turned forwards over the front shape — as in the diagram, and fixed with it at (A) in Fig. 16a. The wing-shapes will remain in position at the sides.

The points at the top of the head can be curled slightly upwards as a decorative feature.

The owls can be mounted against a background or they can be hung freely. If the paper used is stiff enough the claw-like feet can be folded forwards so that the model will stand on a flat surface.

Owl — Teaching Note

A suitable background (representing an old, beamed roof) might be prepared for the owls. Imperial-size sheets of kitchen paper cut in half on the diagonal can be painted with bold patterns to suggest timber, and can be assembled together on a background. Mounted in a large triangular shape the timbers might suggest the interior of a roof, and the owls can be set in places on the beams.

After patterning the owls can be set in various other backgrounds. An area of freely coloured off-cuts can be assembled together to suggest a leafy background. This could be a controlled exercise in, for example, autumn colours.

A different shaped area could be developed as a background with a single tall tree. This could be built up as a symmetrical pattern with strips of dark paper and large painted leaves. The leaves might be given form on a fold or score at the centre, but this type of additional decoration should be done with some restraint, since a background should not be so elaborate that it detracts from the simple visual impact of the shapes it is intended to carry.

Fig. 16b

FROG (1)

Size: Quarter Imperial

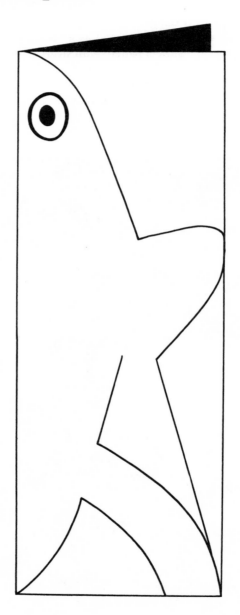

Fig. 17

Drawing the Diagram (Fig. 17)

The top and bottom of this pattern are very similar in shape. Care must be taken to mark the eyes in the right position.

The foot-shapes are included without toes, since these can be cut later and tend to complicate the diagram at this stage.

Raising the Form

Open the shape flat after cutting.

Place it on a flat surface with the outside—on which you have drawn the eyes—face downwards.

Raise the two ends of the paper to meet in the middle at the top (Fig. 17a). Position the eyes as they would be in a real frog.

The front legs will now be sticking out sideways, like the arms of a policeman holding up the traffic. These can be folded forwards into a more natural position—as though the frog, sitting on its haunches, is supporting itself on its front legs as it leans slightly forwards.

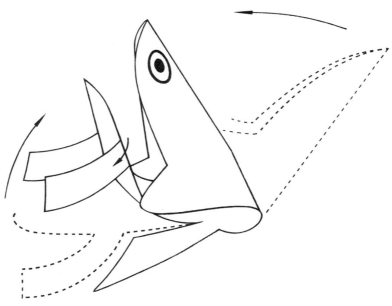

Fig. 17a

The paper between the front legs makes the belly and chest of the frog. When fixing this to the back it must be pulled slightly off-centre at the side before fixing (A) in Fig. 17b. This can be done simply by matching the edges together at the side and then fixing. Before making the second fixture it is again necessary to match the edges together.

This off-centre method of fixing will give form in the back of the frog, since the back shape is wider than the chest and must therefore bulge when the edges are matched together. The form must occur in this instance on the back of the frog where the eyes are painted.

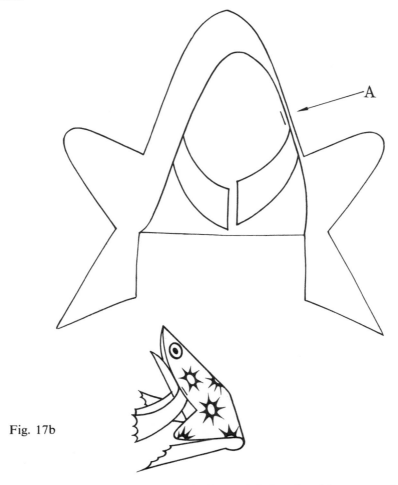

Fig. 17b

Care should be taken when positioning and fixing the sides to see that the curved paper making the lower jaw is set slightly below the top jaw. This difference in the height required by the two sides can be seen in the diagrams.

The frog as you have made it should sit. If it topples over when you place it down you must make slight adjustments to the legs, which can be pinched into the required positions.

At this stage the feet can be cut to look like flippers or toes.

When you can make up the frog you should flatten it again and paint the model on both sides. It can be visually effective to paint the two sides the same colour but in different tones before patterning. But this is a matter of personal choice.

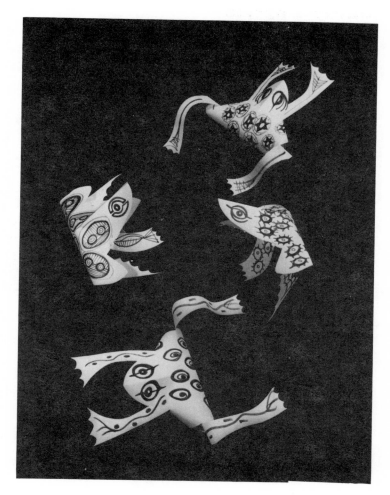

Fig. 17c

FROG (2)

Size: Quarter Imperial

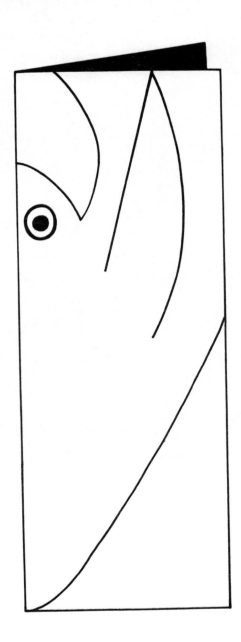

Fig. 18

Drawing the Diagram (Fig. 18)

Care must again be taken to position the eyes at the correct end of the shape.

As in the previous frog the feet are drawn as simple shapes, but in this case they are both at the same end of the diagram.

Raising the Form

As in the previous example, the shape must be opened flat with the eyes underneath. The two sides must again be raised upwards to meet at the top.

The triangular shapes between the legs must be pulled forwards across the body like a waistcoat, and fixed at the crossing point (A) in Fig. 18a. The fixture should be made at the crossing point through three thicknesses of paper – the two side flaps and the chest. The lower jaw should again be positioned a little below the top.

The long back legs of the frog will bend out behind the shape to give it the appearance of a frog about to leap. The legs are fairly flexible and can be positioned at varying angles. This frog, mounted as though it is about to jump, is intended to contrast with the sitting frogs which can be made from the previous pattern.

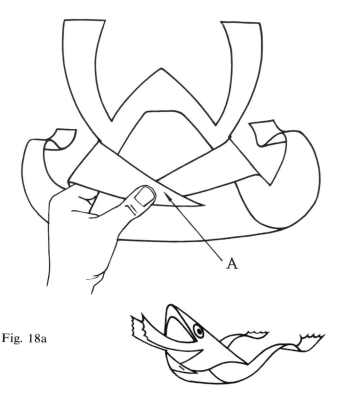

A

Fig. 18a

FROGS – Teaching Note

A watery background for the frogs can be attempted in various ways. Children will probably attempt a watery background by using blue paint and one of the simple fashions or methods with which they are familiar. They might paint wave-like strokes on top of the blue, or they might leave open gaps between their brush strokes. These and other methods are adequate, and might serve very well in the preparation of a background for the frogs.

A more watery effect might, however, be achieved by using a different method. In this case a wax-resist technique might help in making the effect.

On large pieces of kitchen paper of irregular shape pupils can draw a large swimming frog. The frog should be drawn freely and boldly with a piece of ordinary candle which must be rubbed hard on to the paper. The drawing will hardly show as pupils use the candles but they should aim to get a good thick impression in wax on the paper.

A wash of colour – paint with more water than pigment – can be painted over the surface of the paper and all over the wax drawing. The wash can be a very watery blue, but it should be strong enough in colour to register on the background where there is no wax drawing. It will not register on top of the wax.

This wax-resist technique might be very suitable as a background exercise for the frogs, since the swimming shapes might appear in a diffused way beneath the wash, as though they were beneath the surface of the water and slightly distorted in shape.

If the kitchen paper is distributed in odd shapes, and if the pupils attempt to occupy most of the space on their papers with swimming frogs, none of the works will have a precise top or bottom. The background can then be made up as a patchwork of these shapes.

Further work can be attempted by preparing – again on kitchen or thin paper – shapes like floating leaves, which can be patterned and stuck to the background.

Sausage-like shapes cut from waste scraps of paper can be cut and patterned in a dark range of colours to represent bullrushes. These can have stalks made from strips of paper, and can be positioned in and around the background.

The frogs, painted and patterned, can be mounted against the background as a final addition to the project. But the work need not stop at this point.

Flowers or leaves can be prepared and added, or some of the other shapes suggested in the book. The only limits which there are to this type of development are those of the amount of interest which can be sustained by the pupils, or the limiting size of the wall available for mounting the display.

RABBIT

Size: Quarter Imperial

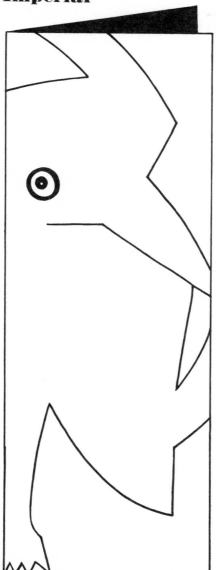

Fig. 19

Drawing the Diagram (Fig. 19)

The front of the rabbit is at the top of the diagram.

The fold will be the backbone of the rabbit, and the section with the eye will bend forward to make the head.

The small shape with V-cuts at the bottom of the diagram is the tail.

The thin shape from the eye to the outer edge of the diagram is the ear. It meets the side at approximately half way.

Raising the Form

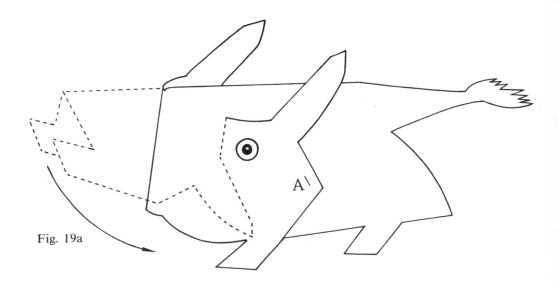

Fig. 19a

Open the shape flat.

The head — the shape on which you have drawn the eyes — can be bent downwards as in Fig. 19a. The arrow shows the direction of movement, and the dotted line the original position of the head. As you move this section downwards the sides should overlap the body, and the ears should stick up slightly above the curve of the back.

The head must be fixed (A) at both sides. These fixtures will cause the back to bend into the type of hunched form which is typical of a rabbit.

Care should be taken when fixing the head to position it with its bottom edge level with the bottom line of the body. This can be seen in the diagram, and will assist in getting the head in the right position before fixing.

The final diagram (19b) illustrates the method of folding the two sides over the centre section. The tail, being on the end of the centre section, will project under the overlapped sides and must be folded upwards after fixing (B).

The rabbit can be completed with toes cut in the feet.

It is a useful shape for an Easter decoration, and can be adapted without much difficulty to make a simple container for family presents.

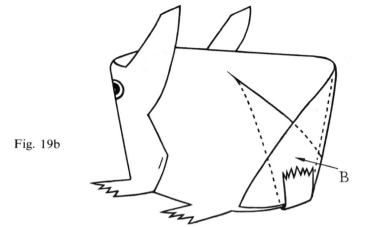

Fig. 19b

B

Fig. 19c

WOODPECKER (1)

Size: Quarter Imperial

Fig. 20

Drawing the Diagram (Fig. 20)

The wing—below the eye-shape—touches the outer edge approximately halfway down the side.

The semi-circular eye-shape is slightly elongated to make fixing easier.

At the bottom of the diagram the shape nearest the fold is the tail. It occupies approximately half of the width.

Raising the Form

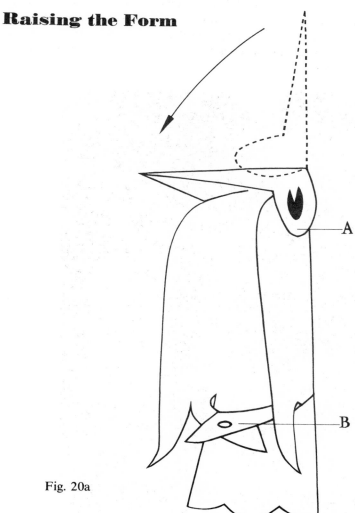

Fig. 20a

Hold the cut shape with the beak pointing upwards.

The top portion—beak and eyes—must be bent downwards until the fold along the top of the beak is horizontal (Fig. 20a). At this stage the eye-shapes must overlap the top of the wing on both sides. These must be fixed in position (A).

This fixture will hold the simple form of the woodpecker, but for mounting, the strips between the bottom of the wing and the sides of the tail should be bent inwards and fixed (B). This fixture can be made with a drawing pin if the woodpecker is to be pinned to a background.

As you will see in the photograph (20b) this is a simple shape—all beak and body—without feet or legs. This is because it is intended to be seen from the sides or back and not from the front. It is a simple and direct shape offering a good opportunity for experiment with colour and pattern, but if the shape is too simple a more advanced model can be made from the next diagram.

Fig. 20b

WOODPECKER (2)

Size: Quarter Imperial

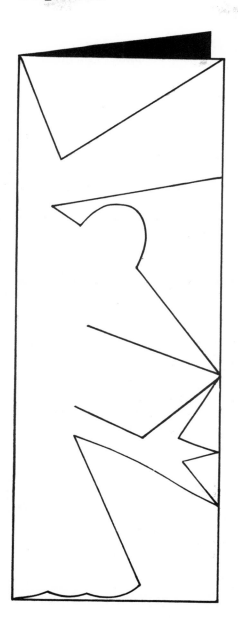

Fig. 21

Drawing the Diagram (Fig. 21)

This is a more advanced model than many of the previous exercises, and the diagram must be studied with that much more care.

Although there is a semi-circular eye-shape in the diagram there is no drawn eye. This is because the eye must be drawn later on the inner side of the paper.

It is desirable that the top part of the diagram should be reproduced as accurately as possible. A little careful work with a ruler will help to establish the correct positioning of various important points in the pattern.

If the model is to be made on the size suggested — Quarter Imperial, 15×11 inches — the pattern will be drawn on half this size — 15×5½ inches, and the following approximate measurements will apply.

Bottom of the beak — 2¾ inches from the top; 1¼ inches from the fold.

This point is joined with lines to the top two corners.

The next point under this is down a further 1¼ inches and is closer to the fold.

The line drawn from this point to the outer edge meets the edge 3¼ inches from the top.

A second line from this point meets the outer edge 8¾ inches from the top. It is this line which carries the semi-circle of the eye.

At this point three other lines also meet the outer edge.

These measurements will assist anyone who wishes to make an accurate reproduction of the pattern. But measuring will not be necessary for those who have developed an ability to see and reproduce proportions reasonably well without the aid of a ruler.

Raising the Form

After cutting, keep the shape folded at the centre.

Fold back the eye- and wing-shape as shown in Fig. 21a. This must be done on both sides. The top point of the fold is at the junction of the eye-shape and the straight line.

Fold the beak forwards and down until the fold of the beak is horizontal, and tuck the long shapes on the beak behind the eye on both sides (21b).

Fix at the bottom point of the wings (B), and make a cylinder-like belly — fixing it at (A) in Fig. 21c.

This is quite an advanced bit of folding, but it should not be too complicated for anyone able to follow the processes stage by stage.

For those who were not successful the first time the process can be repeated from the first stage.

The eye and wing-shapes must be folded back on both sides. The eyes can now be drawn on what was previously the inner side of the paper.

The beak must be folded down into a horizontal position, so that the flap of paper on each side can be tucked behind the eye.

The shapes above the legs make a cylinder at the belly. The form of the woodpecker must be held with two fixtures A & B.

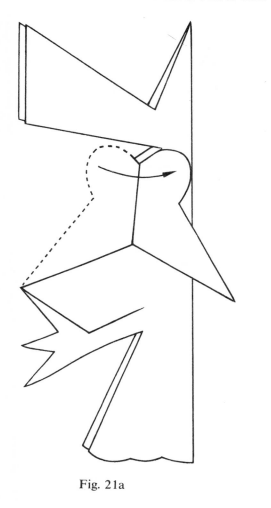

Fig. 21a

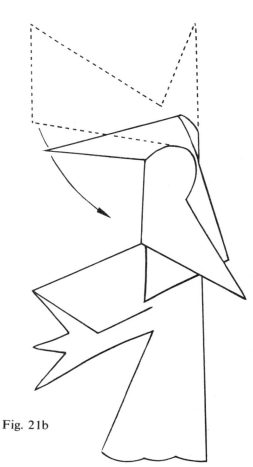

Fig. 21b

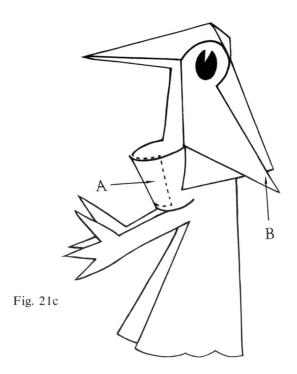

Fig. 21c

Woodpeckers – Teaching Note

Of the two woodpeckers the first shape is obviously likely to be the more suitable for classroom use, although the second can be attempted in careful stages with more able pupils.

For backgrounds trees of various types are most suitable. These can be simple trunk and branch-shapes with large patterned leaves similar to those prepared for previous exercises. But as this type of work is developed with a group, an attempt should be made to make the experience stimulating and different, rather than repetitive. In this instance work on the trees might be experimental.

Half Imperial kitchen paper cut longways (30×11 inches) can be folded into three down its length.

For one exercise the outer strips can be painted in irregular areas of autumn colours, with the centre strip painted all over in round shapes – black with grey centres, giving a mottled effect. Black lines painted down the two folds and enclosing the black and grey pattern can have occasional suggestions of branches painted from it on to the coloured background. These shapes can be mounted together on top of each other, making trees as high as space will allow. They can be crowded together as in a wood, or they can be spaced out.

To vary the exercise, fresh spring-like colours can be used on the outer strips. The inner pattern can be made in dark tones of green.

This is a suggestion for one type of tree. It is a treatment which is different. It is an attempt to experiment with new visual experiences, and is only one of many exercises which can be developed as interesting additions to the work of making and patterning the models.

Other treatments to make trees as a background for the woodpeckers are obviously possible, but as a generally valuable guide the emphasis should be on a patterned rather than a realistic treatment.

Fig. 21d

SWIFT OR SWALLOW

Size: Quarter Imperial

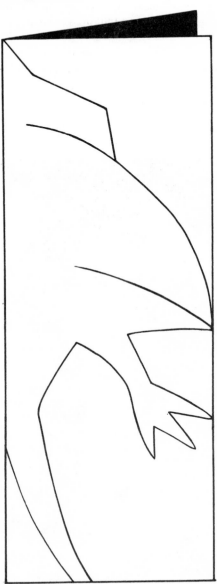

Fig. 22

Drawing the Diagram (Fig. 22)

The pattern is shown without an eye in this instance because the eye is better added after the shape has been made up.

The beak is the pointed shape at the top of the diagram. The single tail-shape at the bottom will make the characteristic double tail when the fold is opened.

The point of the wing touches the outer edge of the pattern a little below the halfway mark.

Raising the Form

Open the shape flat and hold it by one of the flaps at the side of the beak. This flap is a 'return' included to make a fixture possible.

The returns on both sides must be tucked under the front edges of the wings and must be fixed in position (A in Fig. 22a). The eye can be painted at this point of overlap on each side.

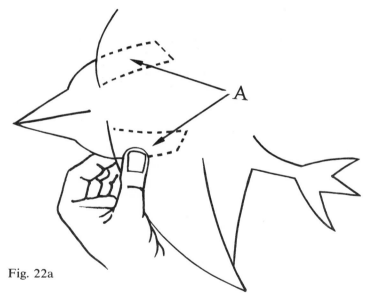

Fig. 22a

The V-shape pieces at the top of the legs can be turned under the shape and over-lapped as a cylinder, making a fixture possible (B in Fig. 22b).

This shape is designed to cling to a background, and the most important parts for patterning are the back and tail.

A number of these birds mounted in a line, some with heads upwards and others down, will look like a row of migrating birds perched on a telephone wire. They will make a pleasant decoration if the decorative treatment is limited to patterns in black and white.

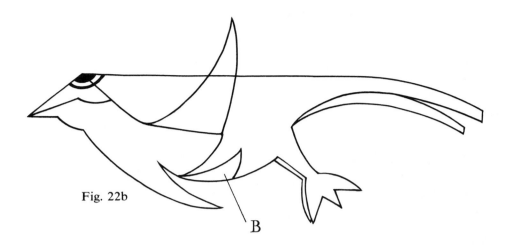

Fig. 22b

B

Swift — Teaching Note

As a contrast to the highly coloured patterns possible with the woodpeckers this shape lends itself to a more restrained treatment. Exercises in black and white are valuable since attention has to be paid to component parts of the pattern.

In this exercise an attempt might be made to relate the pattern to its background shape. A satisfactory pattern often has a simple fluency which is related to the shape. An unsatisfactory pattern might be disjointed and erratic and without any implied or obvious relationship with the shape carrying it.

On a form like the swift it should be possible to see the difference between pattern which fits and pattern which is unrelated to the shape.

Simple horizontal lines make an adequate background for this exercise. These can be drawn directly on a wall, and the birds can be mounted as though they are for some reason perched on the lines.

Where it is not possible to draw or paint directly on the wall, each pupil can begin an exercise with half Imperial kitchen paper cut longways. This can be painted all over one colour to represent the sky. But not necessarily blue. A yellow or an orange sky might make an interesting variation.

After the sky has been painted the paper can be folded across the middle. A black line painted on this fold will be in the same position on every paper, making a single line right across the background when the individual papers are mounted together.

A second black line can be painted across the middle of the lower half on each paper if there are enough birds to perch on two telephone lines.

The bottom quarter of the paper beneath the second line can be filled with a pattern of roof-tops and chimneys. This will add to the visual effect of the end product by suggesting that the birds are perched at a height above the ground. The roof tops and chimneys can be painted in simple black outline.

Fig. 22c

FISH

Size: Quarter Imperial

Fig. 23

Drawing the Diagram (Fig. 23)

The paper is folded in this exercise on its longer side, making in a quarter Imperial sheet an area of 11×7½ inches on each side of the fold.

The top part of the diagram to the left of the eye includes the fold.

Below this the diagram does not touch the fold.

Raising the Form

Open the shape out flat after cutting.

Pick the shape up by its lower edges (see Fig. 23a), and bring the two sides together.

The small triangles beneath the top line of the mouth will turn upwards with this movement so that their lower sides can be matched together.

Fig. 23a

As these triangles are matched the lower sides of the fish will overlap, making a belly under the opening of the mouth. The overlap must be fixed at this point (A in Fig. 23b).

After this fixture has been made the fish will be rather fat and bulky, and it will be open at the back.

The two triangles beneath the tail can be overlapped and fixed (B in Fig. 23c).

Sometimes when form is raised from this pattern the model tends to have its mouth closed. If this is so a gentle pressure on the sides of the fish will cause the mouth to open.

When you are able to make this fish in the size suggested you should try variations in other sizes. The fish can be decorated and hung singly or, if they are made in varying sizes, they can be made up into mobiles (see *Make It in Paper*).*

*Reprinted by Dover (ISBN 0-486-24468-7).

Fig. 23b

Fish – Teaching Note

Fish and undersea themes are popular exercises for colour and pattern work in schools. Exciting and large scale backgrounds can be built up in a number of ways. The fluid nature of an undersea theme is particularly suitable to communal work, and individual contributions of almost any size or shape can be assembled to make an effective background for the fish.

The wax-resist treatment suggested in an earlier exercise might again be used in this instance, with a variety of marine shapes drawn in wax under a wash of suitable colours.

Interesting and effective work can be developed with the use of coloured tissues. These are available in a wide range of colours, and combined with paint will make possible some extremely effective backgrounds.

For this exercise kitchen paper in odd shapes can be painted with simple fish-shapes in various sizes. These should have large white eyes with dark pupils. The kitchen paper can then be covered with coloured tissue, stuck on with powder paste. The use of powder paste is recommended because, used fairly thickly, it will tend to crinkle the tissue and raise interesting textures on the background.

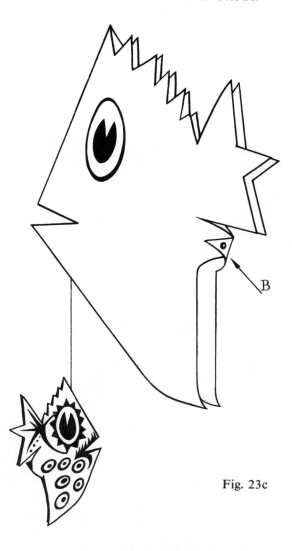

Fig. 23c

For a communal work on a large scale it will be necessary to direct the choice of colour in the tissue used. A predominant colour will unify the finished work, and the effect can then be heightened by the use of further colour and of shapes stuck on top of the tissue. In this way the first painted fish-shapes will appear dimly through the background, giving a watery effect.

Added visual interest is possible with the use of tissue paper on the actual shapes made in this exercise.

At the beginning of the work the quarter Imperial papers might be painted all over in one colour. With more able pupils this might take the form of an exercise involving a change from a light tone at one end to a darker tone at the other. A tissue paper stuck over this might provide a rich effect in colour and texture. When the fish is cut from this and patterned the visual effect will be that much more rewarding than that of a fish made in plain paper.

Fig. 23d

SHARK

Size: Half Imperial (longways 30 × 11 inches)

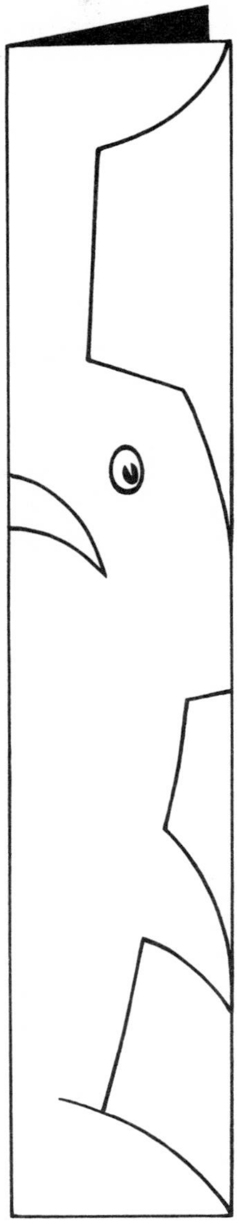

Drawing the Diagram
(Fig. 24)

The crescent-shaped cut in the fold is obviously the mouth. It is slightly above the centre of the fold.

The fold in this model makes the belly of the shark, and it is desirable that the crease of the fold should not be made with too much pressure on the paper. It is really only necessary to fold the paper so that it can be cut double, and by this stage in the work it should be possible to do this without making the fold too emphatic.

Fig. 24

Raising the Form

Open the shape flat after cutting and place it on a surface with the outer side down. The outer side is the one on which the eyes are drawn.

Look at the diagram (Fig. 24a) and see how the head section is raised into a cylinder with the mouth on the under side. This cylinder should be held in position with one hand. The thumb should be at the top at the point marked (A), the forefinger should be inside the cylinder.

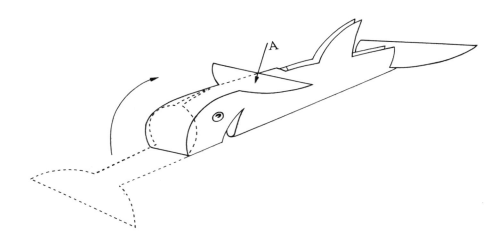

Fig. 24a

With the cylinder held in one hand, that part of the model in front of the head (dotted in diagram) should be raised upwards and backwards to lie along the top of the model. This can be secured together with the sides of the cylinder at (A).

This operation will give you the blunt nose of the shark at the front of the head. The fixture at (A) will hold both this and the curve of the belly in place. If the belly tends to flatten itself out too much at the tail a further fixture can be made through the two dorsal fins at the top of the shark's body.

The tail should retain an almost horizontal position so that it can be seen when the shark is hanging. In order to effect this, the cut of the tail at the front is made into the body.

If you look at the photograph (24b) you will see that the underside with the mouth is the most effective view, and you should mount or hang the sharks with this in mind.

The work you do on this exercise might be combined in a decoration with other marine shapes which you have made in previous exercises.

Fig. 24b

ROUNDABOUT HORSE

Size: Quarter Imperial

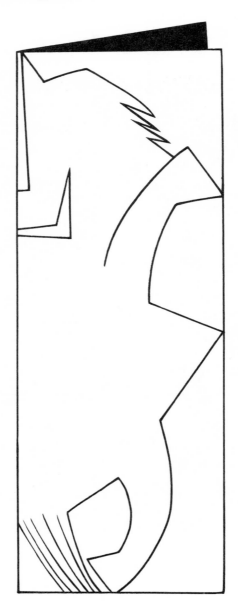

Fig. 25

Drawing the Diagram (Fig. 25)

The back of the horse is along the line of the fold.

At the top of the diagram the front of the head is set slightly away from the fold so that, after cutting, the two sides of the head will be separate except at their lower end.

The pointed section at the middle of the outer edge of the pattern will overlap to make the belly.

The diagram is drawn without an eye because the head must be reversed as the form is raised, and in the finished model the eyes will be on the other side of the paper.

Raising the Form

After cutting, keep the paper folded and match it to Fig. 25a where the dotted line indicates the position of the head.

Fold the head back at the point where it joins the body above the front legs. Repeat on the other side and push the nostril through to the front (small arrow in diagram).

To hold the head in position fix the two sides together at (A). You can now paint in the eyes.

Overlap the cylinder of the belly and fix at (B), giving the body of the horse as much form as possible.

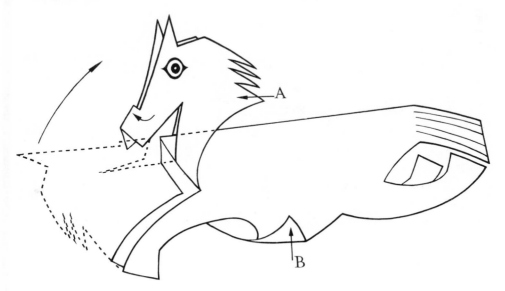

Fig. 25a

Raising this form is actually a very simple operation, although it might be found difficult at a first attempt because the process of raising the two sides of the head is a new one in the work. Before attempting to raise the form it might help to study the photograph (25b) with some care so that the process can be better understood.

After decoration the horses can be hung individually, but they will be more effective if several of them are hung together from a hoop.

Finding the correct point at which to place the cotton in the horse's back should not be difficult with the use of a pin. A pin stuck through the back at a point which seems to be the point of balance will show whether this is in fact so. If the horse tips forwards or backwards the positioning of the pin in the horse's back must be adjusted before the pin-hole can be used for threading the model with cotton.

Fig. 25b

CROCODILE

Size: One third Imperial (22 × 10 inches)

Fig. 26

Drawing the Diagram (Fig. 26)

This is another diagram which must be studied with some care.

On the side of the fold there is only one cut — the pointed shape of the tail. If you are using the size suggested the tail starts on the fold 5½ inches from the bottom and stops 12 inches from the bottom. At its top it is 1¼ inches from the fold.

If the diagram is studied carefully it should be possible to relate the other shapes to this line: the back of the front leg is slightly above it, the front of the rear leg is opposite it.

The lower part of the shape drawn with a jagged edge is the lower jaw of the model, the jagged edge being intended to suggest teeth. At the top of the jagged edge a return is included. You should establish the position of this return because this is the point at which the fixture will be made.

Raising the Form

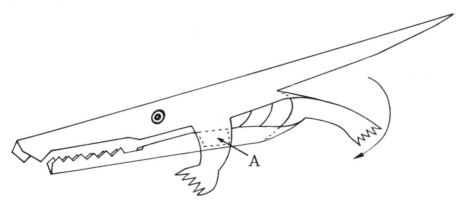

Fig. 26a

Open the shape flat.

With the backbone of the crocodile at the top, bend the shape in two from the base of the tail (see Fig. 26a). The tail must remain straight as that part of the model behind it is turned under to make the belly and lower jaw.

The projecting returns at each side of the lower jaw can be positioned under the front legs on each side and fixed (A).

If you have difficulty in matching the returns with the legs you have probably altered the proportions in some way, and it may be necessary to recut the shape.

Like other shapes the crocodiles can be decorated and mounted as though they are crawling on the walls or ceiling. When you paint a model like this you should remember that it is really intended to amuse and not to terrify.

Fig. 26b

TORTOISE

Size: One third Imperial (22 × 10 inches)

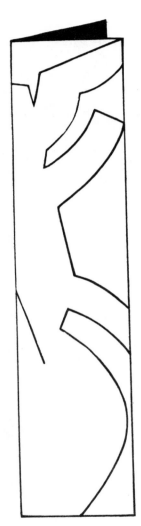

Fig. 27

Drawing the Diagram (Fig. 27)

This diagram is quite advanced and must be studied with particular care before you reproduce it on a larger scale on your paper.

Reading the diagram from the bottom upwards you have the curve of the shell, and above this the back leg.

Nearer the top you have the front leg curving upwards, and then the head.

The cut in the fold which will make the tail is drawn downwards, starting about 10 inches from the bottom. The tail is approximately 3½ inches long.

The eyes can be drawn in after the shape has been made up.

Raising the Form

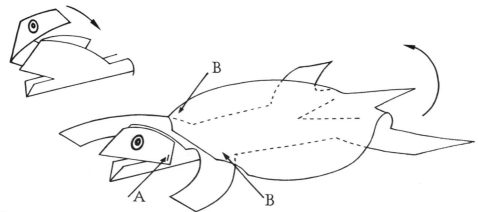

Fig. 27a

Open out flat after cutting, with the fold downwards. The side on which you drew the pattern will be face down.

Look closely at the inset diagram in Fig. 27a and fold the head as shown. Each side of the head must be folded from the point of the nose to the point of the forehead. This will make two similar shapes, one of which must be folded over the other and fixed at the side (A). You can now draw the eye on both sides of the head.

In the crocodile in the previous exercise you bent the form double by folding the back portion down. In this exercise you must again bend the form double, but this time the shape must be bent upwards and forwards until the oval of the shell is positioned evenly on top of the four legs. It can be fixed on both sides at the front legs (B).

When you make this fixture you should try to keep as much form as possible in the back to suggest the raised shell of the tortoise.

Notice that in this case the tail turns upwards from the underside with the oval of the shell.

This is a good exercise for pattern because there is the large area of shell to work on. The models can be painted underneath, but this is not essential since the tortoise is designed to be seen from the top or the sides.

Tortoise — Teaching Note

Suitable backgrounds for this and the previous exercise may be prepared with simple arrangements of colours rather than with representational scenes.

It is an interesting experience to make up a large background from a number of shapes of one colour in a variety of tones. The component shapes can be regular, but of different sizes, in which case — since the same shape is repeated many times — the background will have a certain organisation and balance, both in shape and colour.

As a visual experience this can be contrasted with a background in which the component parts are of mixed and irregular shapes.

The crocodile and the tortoise are both shapes which can be mounted on relatively simple backgrounds, although they can in themselves become vehicles for fairly complicated pattern making.

Fig. 27b

MOUSE

Size: One eighth Imperial (11 × 7½ inches)

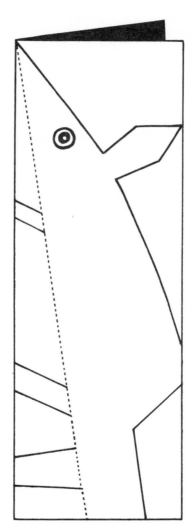

Fig. 28

Drawing the Diagram (Fig. 28)

After folding the paper at the centre make a mark on the bottom edge approximately 1½ inches from the fold.

Do the same on the other side of the fold. This can be done in one operation if scissor points are used to make a very small nick through both sheets at once.

Before drawing the diagram you must fold your paper on both sides from this point at the bottom to the centre top (small dotted lines in diagram). These folds should be made in the same direction as the fold at the centre. It should be possible to see the outside of the paper all the time.

After making the three folds you must return your paper to its original form — with one fold down the centre. The slanting fold, although it will now be flat, will be visible as the dotted line in the diagram.

When you copy the diagram you must include six lines which start at the folded side. In each case these lines stop at the sloping fold which is marked on your paper.

After copying the rest of the diagram as closely as possible, cut the shape and open the paper out flat.

You should have a shape similar to Fig. 28a.

The blacked-in portion (you can shade it in on your own drawing) is not needed in the finished work and must now be cut away. If you cut on the right lines two pieces will fall away from your paper, leaving a pointed shape which tapers from left to right.

Two small vertical cuts must also be made at the centre between the points of the roof-like shapes. The sloping sides of these shapes should already have been cut when you made the six cuts on the lines at the fold of your paper.

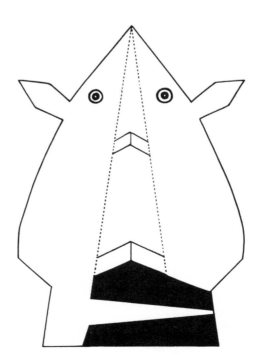

Fig. 28a

Raising the Form

Place the centre triangle down flat.

Raise the two sides on the angled folds—keeping the eyes outwards—and fix them together behind the ears (A in Fig. 28b).

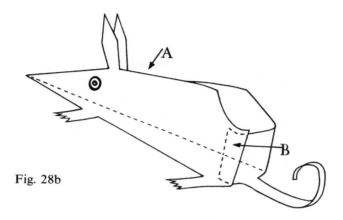

Fig. 28b

Turn the longer side round at the back to overlap the other (see Fig. 28b), and fix at (B). This should bring the tapering tail-shape into the correct position at the rear of the mouse. The tail can be curled slightly.

The four feet can be turned outwards from the flat triangle which is the base of the mouse. You have already cut them.

After you have made up the form there may be a gap at the top of the mouse between the sides. This can be closed by pinning.

After making and decorating the mice you can mount them on any flat surface. It sometimes happens that in this model the triangular base bellies outwards slightly and prevents the shape from standing neatly. If this happens you need only push the base gently up into the body of the mouse so that, instead of projecting down, the middle fold now sticks upwards out of the way.

Mice – Teaching Note

This exercise must be introduced slowly, with the pupils working stage by stage at the teacher's direction. The first mouse will take a little time with children of reasonable ability. But after they have understood the principle they should be able to repeat the process themselves on papers of varying sizes.

The finished and decorated mice can be mounted effectively in any part of the school. It is amusing to have them all apparently running in the same direction but spread out over the largest possible area.

If a prepared background is required it can be developed on several themes. Food on shelves: jars, baskets, packets etc. can be prepared as exercises in colour and pattern. These can be cut out and stuck on a wall in rows — it is not necessary to make the shelves — and the mice can be mounted to run over them.

As a more simple exercise, sacks of flour can be cut from large sheets of old wrapping paper. These can be mounted as though they are stacked in a bakery, and the mice can run over them in all directions.

Fig. 28c

RAT

Size: Half Imperial (longways 30 × 11 inches)

Fig. 29

Drawing the Diagram (Fig. 29)

If you are working to the suggested size the tail in the lower part of your diagram will be about 16 inches long.

This is another diagram in which the eye must be drawn later on the reverse side of the paper.

To understand this diagram it will help to study the making-up diagram and the photograph (29a and b).

Raising the Form

Open the shape flat after cutting.

The narrowest part of the shape is the point of the nose. The portion of paper in front of this must be turned back to make the face. This will be angled from the nose upwards, and fixed into position by the fringe between the ears (A). This fringe must be bent downwards, and the fold at the front of the face must be reversed before you make the fixture.

Form is raised in the body by making the usual overlap at the belly. This is made with the straight sections between the front and back legs, and must be secured at (B).

The back of the rat is folded as in the rabbit, the sides overlapping on top of the tail. A final fixture must be made at this point (C).

To complete the rat the tail can be curled, and toes can be cut in the feet.

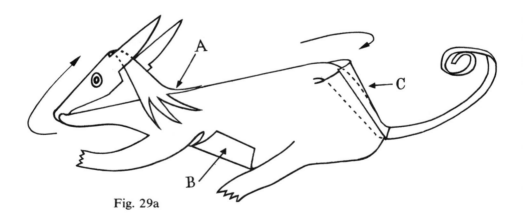

Fig. 29a

Rat – Teaching Note

An interesting project can be developed with a class if this shape is used to illustrate the story of the Pied Piper. Simple cut-out shapes representing the houses of the town can be prepared in gay colours, and can be pasted flat on a wall. When these are mounted they should be positioned together with some partly overlapping others as buildings normally do.

Somewhere in the room the figure of the piper can be a focal point for the rats, which should be coloured all over and patterned.

Fig. 29b

ANGEL

Size: Half Imperial

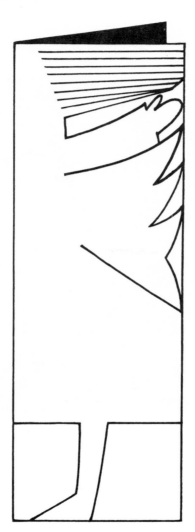

Fig. 30

Drawing the Diagram (Fig. 30)

It is not necessary to reproduce this diagram with absolute accuracy.

The lines close together at the top will make the hair. It is not necessary to count these, since no specific number is required and you can make them thicker or thinner to suit yourself.

Below the hair you will notice the shape of an arm with a simple hand. This is at the top of the wing. The bottom of the wing touches the outer edge of the paper a little below the halfway mark.

The feet at the bottom of the diagram point inwards. They will be in the correct position when the form is raised.

Raising the Form

Fig. 30a

After cutting, open the form and make a cylinder of the skirt—fixing it at (A) in Fig. 30a.

Bend the arms forward to the front of the body, and pinch them at the shoulders to hold them in position.

At this stage the hair is sticking out sideways. It should be bent downwards into a more suitable position and curled.

When drawing the face on the angel you should make it simple with a very small mouth. A large clumsy mouth will tend to make the angel more grotesque than is desirable.

These angel shapes can be decorated and suspended from cottons which may be attached to the models at various points.

If the hands are joined together at the front in a praying gesture, the angels can be effectively mounted on a flat background without having a cylinder made at the skirt. In this case the fold at the centre will support the form which can be pinned to the wall on each side of the skirt.

Fig. 30b

BUTTERFLY
Size: Quarter Imperial

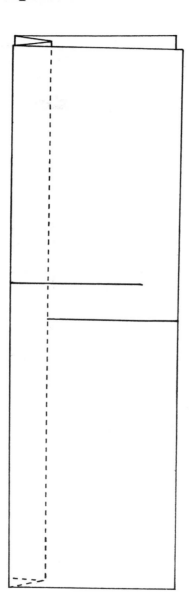

Fig. 31

Drawing the Diagram (Fig. 31)

In this exercise, after making your fold down the middle of the paper, you must fold each side back again about an inch from the centre. You can check that you have done this correctly by comparing your folds with those shown on Fig. 31, or by looking at the end of your paper which should be in the shape of an 'M' with rather long sides.

The only drawing necessary in this model is two straight lines. The first line must be drawn from the outer edge, approximately halfway down its length, to the centre fold. You cannot see the centre fold which is turned back under the surface on which you are drawing, but it should be possible to feel it with your finger.

A second line must be drawn about an inch above this, from the other side (starting at the fold) to within an inch of the outer edge.

These two lines are marked on Fig. 31 in which the centre fold is shown as a dotted line.

Raising the Form

Cut the two horizontal lines.

One of these cuts will be through two thicknesses of paper. The other will begin through four thicknesses and will continue through two.

Open the paper flat with the centre fold upwards in a ridge along the middle.

Pick the paper up, holding it by the smaller length of ridge. This is illustrated in Fig. 31a, in which you can see the paper being lifted by the ridge. When the paper is lifted the larger area will drop and hang in a vertical position.

Still holding the paper by the ridge, you must fold the hanging section upwards to the under surface of the piece you are holding. The movement of this process is shown by the two slightly curved arrows in the diagram.

The centre ridge on the lower portion is now pointing down, and you can tuck the top into it at an angle (see Fig. 31b), fixing it at (A). You should now have a form like the undecorated one in the photograph, 31c.

Make antennae, the feelers which insects have on their heads, by cutting thin strips along the front edges of the model (inset diagram). These can be folded to stick forwards.

The upper and lower wings are rectangular and must now be trimmed at their corners into more suitable shapes.

Although the butterflies are designed to have a certain form, they are suggestions of a shape rather than precise reproductions. You can if you like paint eyes on the lower part of the form at the front, but good painting and decorating are as important as the details of the form. For this reason you should retain as much of the form as possible when you trim the wings, and should not cut away more paper than is necessary.

If you have raised the form of the butterfly and have painted it with suitable pattern and colour, you will see from a distance that fussy details are not necessary. When you hold the form in your hand you will probably want to put in details as they occur to you. You may, of course, do this, but you must expect the smaller details to disappear when you are far enough away from it for your eye to take in the whole shape.

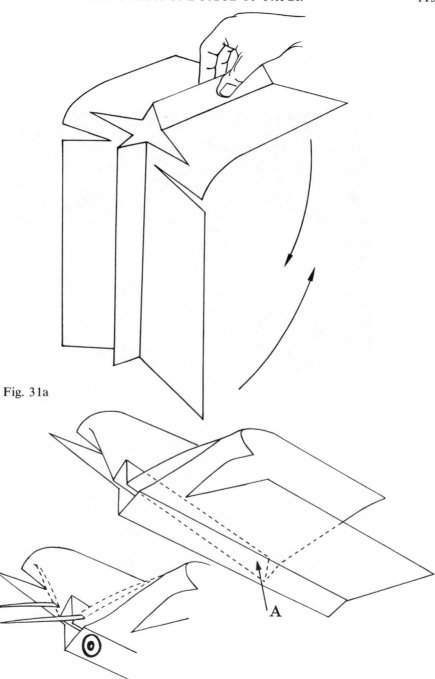

Fig. 31a

Fig. 31b

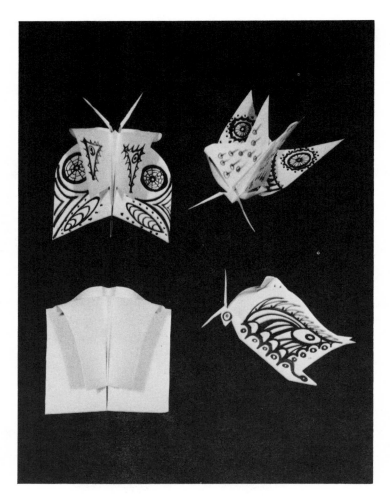

Fig. 31c

CONCLUSION

These are a few of the shapes which lie hidden in a piece of paper.

They are not real. They are make-believe exercises in fantasy from a very ordinary beginning. There are not many things which could be more ordinary or plain than a piece of paper. Nor are there many things which cannot be lifted out of their humdrum state if we use our imagination on them.

If you can picture in your mind a flat piece of paper lying on a bare surface, and can then imagine this same piece of paper rising up into a shape, you should be able to accept the odd forms of some of the exercises.

They are not real things which must be tackled with a frown and with grim determination.

They are games to be played when you feel like it, and they are suggested for your pleasure.

It is inevitable that some of you, on trying the exercises, will grumble because they will be less easy than the diagrams and text would make them appear.

If you meet with difficulty at any point there is no need to worry. You should try again slowly, checking the instructions with the diagrams, and referring to the photographs. You should try to understand the processes which are involved in making the flat paper into a particular shape. You should also look at the paper you are working with, examining it with your eyes and also with your hands. These are the important things.

The book is intended to help you. But it is nothing without your eyes and your hands.

All the shapes suggested are possible.

They have been made by children before you. And in many cases have been adapted and changed in form to suit the people making them. There is no rule against this. If you feel like adapting some of the shapes to suit yourself you must do so.

Better still, if you have made some of the shapes and have developed enough skill and understanding in the process to work out others of your own, you can put aside the book and can concentrate on the piece of paper which you have in your hand.

There is something hidden in it.

If you can find the hidden shape, it does not matter how simple it is, you have reached the stage where you can put away this book.

Books like this are after all written to help beginners.

FOR TEACHERS

The suggestions made in these exercises are offered to those teachers who could use some help in their work with children in art and craft.

The fact that some of these suggestions might be of practical value in certain classroom situations does not imply any criticism of work already going on.

There are in the suggestions some new and possibly interesting opportunities for the development of lessons in which pupils may experiment with pattern and colour.

In order to make the practical work stimulating to the children they are offered interesting shapes. They can break away from the familiar rectangle and can be involved in experiments with new forms.

The work is not complicated or suitable only for the highly skilled specialist. It is rather a number of practical exercises which have been tried in various ways with pupils of a wide range of ability.

In many schools pupils are offered creative opportunities in a wide range of techniques and materials. Teachers in these schools will not need the suggestions made in this book.

But other schools have small rooms and large classes. The pupils must do their creative work in the same rooms in which they do their other subjects, even in the same desks.

The exercises suggested do not need specialist facilities or equipment. The work can be done in the same room as the other subjects, and the pupils can work at their desks. They require only materials which must already be available in all schools.

The work is not intended as a syllabus. Each exercise, used as a vehicle for practical experiment in colour and pattern, can be a work in its own right. Or it can be used as a point of departure for the development of larger projects.

Before using any of the exercises, and before introducing them to the class, interested teachers are recommended to master the shapes themselves.

The use of templates or patterns must be a matter of individual choice. The exercises can be introduced through methodical introduction and blackboard illustration, but some teachers prefer to use templates which they have prepared before the lesson.

A dressmaker using a printed pattern is no less proud of her work because she did not make the pattern. The shapes are offered as interesting opportunities for experiment with colour and pattern. Their incorporation into projects provides further opportunity for the active participation of everyone in the class. Under these circumstances, where it is expedient to prepare and introduce templates, their use is recommended.

Where they are to be used, templates of the shapes are best made in cardboard of suitable durability. Since the forms are all developed on a fold, the templates need only be cut on one side of the shape. They will then incorporate a straight line which will always be placed against the folded edge of the paper.

To assist teachers in the preparation of their lessons each shape was developed originally in size as a simple multiple of a full Imperial sheet (30×22 inches). The teacher who wishes to use an exercise has only to draw paper from stock and tear it to the size suggested.

The exercise can then be introduced, and the children left alone to develop the work in their own way.

Any teacher who takes this book can borrow from it an idea or a suggestion, and can use it as he wishes. The exercises are not designed for a particular age or type of child, and the teacher must expect to adapt or modify them to suit the situation.

For very young children it might be necessary to cut and decorate only very simple shapes. They might be encouraged to cut leaf shapes as large as possible. After painting, these could be pinned to the wall as a basis for further simple experiment. The children could try cutting snails or birds—simple flat shapes with two eyes and a beak. These and simple versions of other creatures could be coloured and pinned to the original leaves. A number of children in a group could cut parts of a caterpillar, or the individual petals of very large flowers. If there are leaves and flowers or buds and seeds in the classroom, and the children can handle these, they might begin to see shapes which are new or shapes which they can recreate in their own way. This does not have to involve any formal study of the objects. Patterns, colours and shapes are around us every day, and the more children are encouraged to look at them the more they may discover about the visual excitement of the world in which we live.

The basic object of the exercises at any level is to provide children with simple and new creative opportunities which can be attempted in readily available materials. In this way they might be assisted towards finding something in which they can be interested and actively involved, which is how we like our children best—interested and actively involved.

A CATALOG OF SELECTED
DOVER BOOKS
IN ALL FIELDS OF INTEREST

A CATALOG OF SELECTED DOVER
BOOKS IN ALL FIELDS OF INTEREST

CONCERNING THE SPIRITUAL IN ART, Wassily Kandinsky. Pioneering work by father of abstract art. Thoughts on color theory, nature of art. Analysis of earlier masters. 12 illustrations. 80pp. of text. 5⅜ × 8½.   23411-8 Pa. $3.95

ANIMALS: 1,419 Copyright-Free Illustrations of Mammals, Birds, Fish, Insects, etc., Jim Harter (ed.). Clear wood engravings present, in extremely lifelike poses, over 1,000 species of animals. One of the most extensive pictorial sourcebooks of its kind. Captions. Index. 284pp. 9 × 12.   23766-4 Pa. $12.95

CELTIC ART: The Methods of Construction, George Bain. Simple geometric techniques for making Celtic interlacements, spirals, Kells-type initials, animals, humans, etc. Over 500 illustrations. 160pp. 9 × 12. (USO)   22923-8 Pa. $9.95

AN ATLAS OF ANATOMY FOR ARTISTS, Fritz Schider. Most thorough reference work on art anatomy in the world. Hundreds of illustrations, including selections from works by Vesalius, Leonardo, Goya, Ingres, Michelangelo, others. 593 illustrations. 192pp. 7⅛ × 10¼.   20241-0 Pa. $9.95

CELTIC HAND STROKE-BY-STROKE (Irish Half-Uncial from "The Book of Kells"): An Arthur Baker Calligraphy Manual, Arthur Baker. Complete guide to creating each letter of the alphabet in distinctive Celtic manner. Covers hand position, strokes, pens, inks, paper, more. Illustrated. 48pp. 8¼ × 11.
     24336-2 Pa. $3.95

EASY ORIGAMI, John Montroll. Charming collection of 32 projects (hat, cup, pelican, piano, swan, many more) specially designed for the novice origami hobbyist. Clearly illustrated easy-to-follow instructions insure that even beginning papercrafters will achieve successful results. 48pp. 8¼ × 11.   27298-2 Pa. $2.95

THE COMPLETE BOOK OF BIRDHOUSE CONSTRUCTION FOR WOOD-WORKERS, Scott D. Campbell. Detailed instructions, illustrations, tables. Also data on bird habitat and instinct patterns. Bibliography. 3 tables. 63 illustrations in 15 figures. 48pp. 5¼ × 8½.   24407-5 Pa. $1.95

BLOOMINGDALE'S ILLUSTRATED 1886 CATALOG: Fashions, Dry Goods and Housewares, Bloomingdale Brothers. Famed merchants' extremely rare catalog depicting about 1,700 products: clothing, housewares, firearms, dry goods, jewelry, more. Invaluable for dating, identifying vintage items. Also, copyright-free graphics for artists, designers. Co-published with Henry Ford Museum & Green-field Village. 160pp. 8¼ × 11.   25780-0 Pa. $9.95

HISTORIC COSTUME IN PICTURES, Braun & Schneider. Over 1,450 costumed figures in clearly detailed engravings—from dawn of civilization to end of 19th century. Captions. Many folk costumes. 256pp. 8⅜ × 11¾.   23150-X Pa. $11.95

FRANK LLOYD WRIGHT'S HOLLYHOCK HOUSE, Donald Hoffmann. Lavishly illustrated, carefully documented study of one of Wright's most controversial residential designs. Over 120 photographs, floor plans, elevations, etc. Detailed perceptive text by noted Wright scholar. Index. 128pp. 9¼ × 10¾.
27133-1 Pa. $11.95

THE MALE AND FEMALE FIGURE IN MOTION: 60 Classic Photographic Sequences, Eadweard Muybridge. 60 true-action photographs of men and women walking, running, climbing, bending, turning, etc., reproduced from rare 19th-century masterpiece. vi + 121pp. 9 × 12. 24745-7 Pa. $10.95

1001 QUESTIONS ANSWERED ABOUT THE SEASHORE, N. J. Berrill and Jacquelyn Berrill. Queries answered about dolphins, sea snails, sponges, starfish, fishes, shore birds, many others. Covers appearance, breeding, growth, feeding, much more. 305pp. 5¼ × 8¼. 23366-9 Pa. $7.95

GUIDE TO OWL WATCHING IN NORTH AMERICA, Donald S. Heintzelman. Superb guide offers complete data and descriptions of 19 species: barn owl, screech owl, snowy owl, many more. Expert coverage of owl-watching equipment, conservation, migrations and invasions, etc. Guide to observing sites. 84 illustrations. xiii + 193pp. 5⅜ × 8½. 27344-X Pa. $8.95

MEDICINAL AND OTHER USES OF NORTH AMERICAN PLANTS: A Historical Survey with Special Reference to the Eastern Indian Tribes, Charlotte Erichsen-Brown. Chronological historical citations document 500 years of usage of plants, trees, shrubs native to eastern Canada, northeastern U.S. Also complete identifying information. 343 illustrations. 544pp. 6½ × 9¼. 25951-X Pa. $12.95

STORYBOOK MAZES, Dave Phillips. 23 stories and mazes on two-page spreads: Wizard of Oz, Treasure Island, Robin Hood, etc. Solutions. 64pp. 8¼ × 11.
23628-5 Pa. $2.95

NEGRO FOLK MUSIC, U.S.A., Harold Courlander. Noted folklorist's scholarly yet readable analysis of rich and varied musical tradition. Includes authentic versions of over 40 folk songs. Valuable bibliography and discography. xi + 324pp. 5⅜ × 8½. 27350-4 Pa. $7.95

MOVIE-STAR PORTRAITS OF THE FORTIES, John Kobal (ed.). 163 glamor, studio photos of 106 stars of the 1940s: Rita Hayworth, Ava Gardner, Marlon Brando, Clark Gable, many more. 176pp. 8⅜ × 11¼. 23546-7 Pa. $11.95

BENCHLEY LOST AND FOUND, Robert Benchley. Finest humor from early 30s, about pet peeves, child psychologists, post office and others. Mostly unavailable elsewhere. 73 illustrations by Peter Arno and others. 183pp. 5⅜ × 8½.
22410-4 Pa. $5.95

YEKL and THE IMPORTED BRIDEGROOM AND OTHER STORIES OF YIDDISH NEW YORK, Abraham Cahan. Film Hester Street based on Yekl (1896). Novel, other stories among first about Jewish immigrants on N.Y.'s East Side. 240pp. 5⅜ × 8½. 22427-9 Pa. $6.95

SELECTED POEMS, Walt Whitman. Generous sampling from *Leaves of Grass*. Twenty-four poems include "I Hear America Singing," "Song of the Open Road," "I Sing the Body Electric," "When Lilacs Last in the Dooryard Bloom'd," "O Captain! My Captain!"—all reprinted from an authoritative edition. Lists of titles and first lines. 128pp. 5$\frac{3}{16}$ × 8¼. 26878-0 Pa. $1.00

MY BONDAGE AND MY FREEDOM, Frederick Douglass. Born a slave, Douglass became outspoken force in antislavery movement. The best of Douglass' autobiographies. Graphic description of slave life. 464pp. 5⅜ × 8½.   22457-0 Pa. $8.95

FOLLOWING THE EQUATOR: A Journey Around the World, Mark Twain. Fascinating humorous account of 1897 voyage to Hawaii, Australia, India, New Zealand, etc. Ironic, bemused reports on peoples, customs, climate, flora and fauna, politics, much more. 197 illustrations. 720pp. 5⅜ × 8½.   26113-1 Pa. $15.95

THE PEOPLE CALLED SHAKERS, Edward D. Andrews. Definitive study of Shakers: origins, beliefs, practices, dances, social organization, furniture and crafts, etc. 33 illustrations. 351pp. 5⅜ × 8½.   21081-2 Pa. $8.95

THE MYTHS OF GREECE AND ROME, H. A. Guerber. A classic of mythology, generously illustrated, long prized for its simple, graphic, accurate retelling of the principal myths of Greece and Rome, and for its commentary on their origins and significance. With 64 illustrations by Michelangelo, Raphael, Titian, Rubens, Canova, Bernini and others. 480pp. 5⅜ × 8½.   27584-1 Pa. $9.95

PSYCHOLOGY OF MUSIC, Carl E. Seashore. Classic work discusses music as a medium from psychological viewpoint. Clear treatment of physical acoustics, auditory apparatus, sound perception, development of musical skills, nature of musical feeling, host of other topics. 88 figures. 408pp. 5⅜ × 8½.   21851-1 Pa. $9.95

THE PHILOSOPHY OF HISTORY, Georg W. Hegel. Great classic of Western thought develops concept that history is not chance but rational process, the evolution of freedom. 457pp. 5⅜ × 8½.   20112-0 Pa. $9.95

THE BOOK OF TEA, Kakuzo Okakura. Minor classic of the Orient: entertaining, charming explanation, interpretation of traditional Japanese culture in terms of tea ceremony. 94pp. 5⅜ × 8½.   20070-1 Pa. $3.95

LIFE IN ANCIENT EGYPT, Adolf Erman. Fullest, most thorough, detailed older account with much not in more recent books, domestic life, religion, magic, medicine, commerce, much more. Many illustrations reproduce tomb paintings, carvings, hieroglyphs, etc. 597pp. 5⅜ × 8½.   22632-8 Pa. $10.95

SUNDIALS, Their Theory and Construction, Albert Waugh. Far and away the best, most thorough coverage of ideas, mathematics concerned, types, construction, adjusting anywhere. Simple, nontechnical treatment allows even children to build several of these dials. Over 100 illustrations. 230pp. 5⅜ × 8½.   22947-5 Pa. $7.95

DYNAMICS OF FLUIDS IN POROUS MEDIA, Jacob Bear. For advanced students of ground water hydrology, soil mechanics and physics, drainage and irrigation engineering, and more. 335 illustrations. Exercises, with answers. 784pp. 6⅛ × 9¼.   65675-6 Pa. $19.95

SONGS OF EXPERIENCE: Facsimile Reproduction with 26 Plates in Full Color, William Blake. 26 full-color plates from a rare 1826 edition. Includes "The Tyger," "London," "Holy Thursday," and other poems. Printed text of poems. 48pp. 5¼ × 7.   24636-1 Pa. $4.95

OLD-TIME VIGNETTES IN FULL COLOR, Carol Belanger Grafton (ed.). Over 390 charming, often sentimental illustrations, selected from archives of Victorian graphics—pretty women posing, children playing, food, flowers, kittens and puppies, smiling cherubs, birds and butterflies, much more. All copyright-free. 48pp. 9¼ × 12¼.   27269-9 Pa. $5.95

PERSPECTIVE FOR ARTISTS, Rex Vicat Cole. Depth, perspective of sky and sea, shadows, much more, not usually covered. 391 diagrams, 81 reproductions of drawings and paintings. 279pp. 5⅜ × 8½. 22487-2 Pa. $6.95

DRAWING THE LIVING FIGURE, Joseph Sheppard. Innovative approach to artistic anatomy focuses on specifics of surface anatomy, rather than muscles and bones. Over 170 drawings of live models in front, back and side views, and in widely varying poses. Accompanying diagrams. 177 illustrations. Introduction. Index. 144pp. 8⅜ × 11¼. 26723-7 Pa. $8.95

GOTHIC AND OLD ENGLISH ALPHABETS: 100 Complete Fonts, Dan X. Solo. Add power, elegance to posters, signs, other graphics with 100 stunning copyright-free alphabets: Blackstone, Dolbey, Germania, 97 more—including many lower-case, numerals, punctuation marks. 104pp. 8⅛ × 11. 24695-7 Pa. $8.95

HOW TO DO BEADWORK, Mary White. Fundamental book on craft from simple projects to five-bead chains and woven works. 106 illustrations. 142pp. 5⅜ × 8. 20697-1 Pa. $4.95

THE BOOK OF WOOD CARVING, Charles Marshall Sayers. Finest book for beginners discusses fundamentals and offers 34 designs. "Absolutely first rate . . . well thought out and well executed."—E. J. Tangerman. 118pp. 7¾ × 10⅝. 23654-4 Pa. $5.95

ILLUSTRATED CATALOG OF CIVIL WAR MILITARY GOODS: Union Army Weapons, Insignia, Uniform Accessories, and Other Equipment, Schuyler, Hartley, and Graham. Rare, profusely illustrated 1846 catalog includes Union Army uniform and dress regulations, arms and ammunition, coats, insignia, flags, swords, rifles, etc. 226 illustrations. 160pp. 9 × 12. 24939-5 Pa. $10.95

WOMEN'S FASHIONS OF THE EARLY 1900s: An Unabridged Republication of "New York Fashions, 1909," National Cloak & Suit Co. Rare catalog of mail-order fashions documents women's and children's clothing styles shortly after the turn of the century. Captions offer full descriptions, prices. Invaluable resource for fashion, costume historians. Approximately 725 illustrations. 128pp. 8⅜ × 11¼. 27276-1 Pa. $11.95

THE 1912 AND 1915 GUSTAV STICKLEY FURNITURE CATALOGS, Gustav Stickley. With over 200 detailed illustrations and descriptions, these two catalogs are essential reading and reference materials and identification guides for Stickley furniture. Captions cite materials, dimensions and prices. 112pp. 6½ × 9¼. 26676-1 Pa. $9.95

EARLY AMERICAN LOCOMOTIVES, John H. White, Jr. Finest locomotive engravings from early 19th century: historical (1804–74), main-line (after 1870), special, foreign, etc. 147 plates. 142pp. 11⅜ × 8¼. 22772-3 Pa. $10.95

THE TALL SHIPS OF TODAY IN PHOTOGRAPHS, Frank O. Braynard. Lavishly illustrated tribute to nearly 100 majestic contemporary sailing vessels: Amerigo Vespucci, Clearwater, Constitution, Eagle, Mayflower, Sea Cloud, Victory, many more. Authoritative captions provide statistics, background on each ship. 190 black-and-white photographs and illustrations. Introduction. 128pp. 8⅞ × 11¾. 27163-3 Pa. $13.95

EARLY NINETEENTH-CENTURY CRAFTS AND TRADES, Peter Stockham (ed.). Extremely rare 1807 volume describes to youngsters the crafts and trades of the day: brickmaker, weaver, dressmaker, bookbinder, ropemaker, saddler, many more. Quaint prose, charming illustrations for each craft. 20 black-and-white line illustrations. 192pp. 4⅝ × 6. 27293-1 Pa. $4.95

VICTORIAN FASHIONS AND COSTUMES FROM HARPER'S BAZAR, 1867–1898, Stella Blum (ed.). Day costumes, evening wear, sports clothes, shoes, hats, other accessories in over 1,000 detailed engravings. 320pp. 9⅜ × 12¼.
22990-4 Pa. $13.95

GUSTAV STICKLEY, THE CRAFTSMAN, Mary Ann Smith. Superb study surveys broad scope of Stickley's achievement, especially in architecture. Design philosophy, rise and fall of the Craftsman empire, descriptions and floor plans for many Craftsman houses, more. 86 black-and-white halftones. 31 line illustrations. Introduction. 208pp. 6½ × 9¼. 27210-9 Pa. $9.95

THE LONG ISLAND RAIL ROAD IN EARLY PHOTOGRAPHS, Ron Ziel. Over 220 rare photos, informative text document origin (1844) and development of rail service on Long Island. Vintage views of early trains, locomotives, stations, passengers, crews, much more. Captions. 8⅞ × 11¾. 26301-0 Pa. $13.95

THE BOOK OF OLD SHIPS: From Egyptian Galleys to Clipper Ships, Henry B. Culver. Superb, authoritative history of sailing vessels, with 80 magnificent line illustrations. Galley, bark, caravel, longship, whaler, many more. Detailed, informative text on each vessel by noted naval historian. Introduction. 256pp. 5⅜ × 8½. 27332-6 Pa. $6.95

TEN BOOKS ON ARCHITECTURE, Vitruvius. The most important book ever written on architecture. Early Roman aesthetics, technology, classical orders, site selection, all other aspects. Morgan translation. 331pp. 5⅜ × 8½. 20645-9 Pa. $8.95

THE HUMAN FIGURE IN MOTION, Eadweard Muybridge. More than 4,500 stopped-action photos, in action series, showing undraped men, women, children jumping, lying down, throwing, sitting, wrestling, carrying, etc. 390pp. 7⅞ × 10⅝.
20204-6 Clothbd. $24.95

TREES OF THE EASTERN AND CENTRAL UNITED STATES AND CANADA, William M. Harlow. Best one-volume guide to 140 trees. Full descriptions, woodlore, range, etc. Over 600 illustrations. Handy size. 288pp. 4½ × 6⅜.
20395-6 Pa. $5.95

SONGS OF WESTERN BIRDS, Dr. Donald J. Borror. Complete song and call repertoire of 60 western species, including flycatchers, juncoes, cactus wrens, many more—includes fully illustrated booklet. Cassette and manual 99913-0 $8.95

GROWING AND USING HERBS AND SPICES, Milo Miloradovich. Versatile handbook provides all the information needed for cultivation and use of all the herbs and spices available in North America. 4 illustrations. Index. Glossary. 236pp. 5⅜ × 8½. 25058-X Pa. $6.95

BIG BOOK OF MAZES AND LABYRINTHS, Walter Shepherd. 50 mazes and labyrinths in all—classical, solid, ripple, and more—in one great volume. Perfect inexpensive puzzler for clever youngsters. Full solutions. 112pp. 8⅛ × 11.
22951-3 Pa. $4.95

THE INFLUENCE OF SEA POWER UPON HISTORY, 1660–1783, A. T. Mahan. Influential classic of naval history and tactics still used as text in war colleges. First paperback edition. 4 maps. 24 battle plans. 640pp. 5⅜ × 8½.
25509-3 Pa. $12.95

THE STORY OF THE TITANIC AS TOLD BY ITS SURVIVORS, Jack Winocour (ed.). What it was really like. Panic, despair, shocking inefficiency, and a little heroism. More thrilling than any fictional account. 26 illustrations. 320pp. 5⅜ × 8½.
20610-6 Pa. $8.95

FAIRY AND FOLK TALES OF THE IRISH PEASANTRY, William Butler Yeats (ed.). Treasury of 64 tales from the twilight world of Celtic myth and legend: "The Soul Cages," "The Kildare Pooka," "King O'Toole and his Goose," many more. Introduction and Notes by W. B. Yeats. 352pp. 5⅜ × 8½.
26941-8 Pa. $8.95

BUDDHIST MAHAYANA TEXTS, E. B. Cowell and Others (eds.). Superb, accurate translations of basic documents in Mahayana Buddhism, highly important in history of religions. The Buddha-karita of Asvaghosha, Larger Sukhavativyuha, more. 448pp. 5⅜ × 8½. ,
25552-2 Pa. $9.95

ONE TWO THREE . . . INFINITY: Facts and Speculations of Science, George Gamow. Great physicist's fascinating, readable overview of contemporary science: number theory, relativity, fourth dimension, entropy, genes, atomic structure, much more. 128 illustrations. Index. 352pp. 5⅜ × 8½.
25664-2 Pa. $8.95

ENGINEERING IN HISTORY, Richard Shelton Kirby, et al. Broad, nontechnical survey of history's major technological advances: birth of Greek science, industrial revolution, electricity and applied science, 20th-century automation, much more. 181 illustrations. ". . . excellent . . ."—Isis. Bibliography. vii + 530pp. 5⅜ × 8¼.
26412-2 Pa. $14.95

Prices subject to change without notice.

Available at your book dealer or write for free catalog to Dept. GI, Dover Publications, Inc., 31 East 2nd St., Mineola, N.Y. 11501. Dover publishes more than 500 books each year on science, elementary and advanced mathematics, biology, music, art, literary history, social sciences and other areas.